942.493

B R I T A I N   I N   O L D   P H O T O G R A P H S

D1556503

NETHERTON
PEOPLE & PLACES

NED WILLIAMS

First published 2008

The History Press
The Mill, Brimscmbe Port,
Stroud, Gloucestershire, GL5 2QG
www.thehistorypress.co.uk

Reprinted 2009

Title page photograph: A Netherton
postcard produced by R.A.P. & Co.
in their 'Latest Photographs' series.
(*Megan Crofts*)

British Library Cataloguing in Publication Data
A catalogue record for this book is available from the
British Library.

ISBN 978-07509-4666-7

Typeset in 10.5/13.5 Photina.
Typesetting and origination by
The History Press.
Printed and bound in England.

THE BLACK COUNTRY SOCIETY

The Black Country Society is proud to be associated with **Sutton Publishing** of Stroud. In 1994 the society was invited by Sutton Publishing to collaborate in what has proved to be a highly successful publishing partnership, namely the extension of the *Britain in Old Photographs* series into the Black Country. In this joint venture the Black Country Society has played an important role in establishing and developing a major contribution to the region's photographic archives by encouraging society members to compile books of photographs of the area or town in which they live.

The first book in the Black Country series was *Wednesbury in Old Photographs* by Ian Bott, launched by Lord Archer of Sandwell in November 1994. Since then almost 70 Black Country titles have been published. The total number of photographs contained in these books is in excess of 13,000, suggesting that the whole collection is probably the largest regional photographic survey of its type in any part of the country to date.

This voluntary society was founded in 1967 as a reaction to the trends of the late 1950s and early '60s. This was a time when the reorganisation of local government was seen as a threat to the identity of individual communities and when, in the name of progress and modernisation, the industrial heritage of the Black Country was in danger of being swept away.

The general aims of the society are to stimulate interest in the past, present and future of the Black Country, and to secure at regional and national levels an accurate understanding and portrayal of what constitutes the Black Country and, wherever possible, to encourage and facilitate the preservation of the Black Country's heritage.

The society, which now has over 2,500 members worldwide, organises a yearly programme of activities. There are six venues in the Black Country where evening meetings are held on a monthly basis from September to April. In the summer months, there are fortnightly guided evening walks in the Black Country and its green borderland, and there is also a full programme of excursions further afield by car. Details of all these activities are to be found on the society's website, **www.blackcountrysociety.co.uk**, and in *The Blackcountryman*, the quarterly magazine that is distributed to all members.

PO Box 71 · Kingswinford · West Midlands DY6 9YN

CONTENTS

Just before the First World War Thomas Jackson of Wolverhampton submitted plans to build a cinema in Netherton High Street. Had this been built would it have added to the status of High Street at the expense of Halesowen Road?

When Mark Washington Fletcher wrote his history of Netherton he called it *From Edward to Edward*, signifying that the township had a history that stretched from medieval times to important events of the twentieth century. The important event of the twentieth century to which his title referred was Netherton's famous royal visit on 6 May 1923 when Edward, Prince of Wales, came to the Black Country. Here we see the prince visiting Noah Hingley's iron works in Netherton. The prince is wearing a black bowler hat. Facing him is the Mayor of Dudley, Cllr Tanfield, and with his back to the camera is Barney Norton, local councillor and secretary of the Iron and Steel Workers' Union. Prince Edward was presented with a silver model chain and anchor by Ben Hodgetts, aged seventy-three. Ben had worked at Hingley's for sixty years and had no intention of retiring. The prince was also offered a whippet as a memento of the Black Country, but he declined the offer. By the end of the week in which the visit took place, a film of the event was being screened at Dudley's Empire cinema in Hall Street. (*Megan Crofts*)

INTRODUCTION

Welcome to the second collection of photographs of Netherton. Hopefully you will have seen the first collection – published in 2006 as *Netherton in Old Photographs* – to which this is the sequel. Occasionally you will find cross-references to the first volume in the captions in this book, and you will also find a map at the beginning of the first book so each book complements the other.

The majority of readers will be very familiar with Netherton and therefore the town possibly needs little introduction, but as a 'furriner' myself, I sympathise with those who need a little help in coming to know Netherton. The basic problem for an outsider trying to make sense of the Black Country is to comprehend how the region forever breaks down into smaller and smaller components. At first this task looks easy as the Black Country is now neatly divided into four administrative units – three metropolitan boroughs and a city. It becomes a little more complicated as we take each of these in turn and find that their 1974 boundaries involved roping together a number of towns that previously enjoyed quite a separate existence. For example, when we look at the modern metropolitan borough of Dudley we find that its has had to embrace places like Stourbridge, Halesowen and Brierley Hill. So where does Netherton come into all this?

Halesowen Road in the centre of Netherton, *c.* 1980. This is probably the most photographed part of Netherton and the most striking example of how the urban landscape continually changes. The Co-op has become the post office, Robinson's has become Firkin's, the wine store has lost its black and white vitrolite frontage and Pricerite has become Spar. Even the bus shelter has been modernised. *(NW)*

When the Borough of Dudley was created in 1865 it included the neighbouring village of Netherton within its boundary. In that sense Netherton is no different to other sub-sections of Dudley, like Eve Hill, Kates Hill, Holly Hall, etc. However, I would argue that it does feel different – much more like an independent township with its own boundaries and sense of identity. Perhaps that was recognised by the fairly early creation of Netherton as a separate parish in 1844, fourteen years after the opening of St Andrew's Church. The other suburbs of Dudley did not become parishes until later in the nineteenth century. Certainly, by the end of the nineteenth century Netherton was remarkably self-contained and had more amenities than some of the surrounding autonomous urban districts.

Having divided Dudley into parts and recognised the separate identity of Netherton, the process of sub-dividing the Black Country does not end. It is possible to continue the process by dividing Netherton into its parts. In this book I try to recognise the identity of places like Dudley Wood and Darby End, but there are many other components of Netherton that might feel they deserve individual attention, such as Baptist End, Cinder Bank, Windmill End, Primrose Hill, Lodge Farm, the Yew Tree Hills and Saltwells. For the time being they will have to be content with being lumped together as Netherton, but each deserve to have their history told in more detail in the future.

Do you have any photos of Netherton? is a question I frequently ask. Often people only keep pictures of friends and family, but even these pictures may show some aspect of a town's past, a section of street or a corner of a building otherwise unrecorded. Sometimes all local history seems to consist of such glimpses of the past. Ann Phipps and Donald Harris stand outside 14 Double Row, Darby End, looking towards Oak Street in the late 1930s. (*Jack Phipps Collection*)

The more one studies Netherton the more apparent it becomes that the first phase of transforming the local landscape has been largely obliterated by later phases. It is now difficult to imagine the number of small pits that covered vast areas during the first half of the nineteenth century, or imagine the landscape through which the canals were built and the village began to grow. We do have detailed Ordnance Survey maps and we must be grateful that Alan Godfrey has reprinted many of the turn-of-the-century maps to give us a picture of that legacy. The legacy on the ground has been subsidence. Subsidence meant that much of the old Netherton fell down or had to be replaced in the early twentieth century. Chapels had to be rebuilt and sections of the centre of the village had to be replaced. However, renewal only took place where circumstances dictated and by the middle of the twentieth century Netherton was an interesting mixture of the old and the not quite so old. Add to that the developments that have taken place since the middle of the twentieth century and we have the very complex landscape that now forms today's Netherton.

The development of Netherton produced the community's own elite of coalmasters and ironmasters etc., and for a time the various social classes of Netherton lived in close proximity to one another. A network of social interaction developed around church and chapel, pubs, clubs and friendly societies. All this created a vibrant community that is difficult to imagine in this rather home-centred age. The photographs reflect this and stir up nostalgia for the Netherton of the past.

The quest for old photographs often leads to school photos – visual chronicles of the hundreds of children who grew up in the area under inspection. Here is Mr Milton's class at Northfield Road Junior School in about 1960. Back row, left to right: Doreen Mole, Janice Evans, Sheridan Hughes, Gillian Blair, -?-, Janet Davies. Middle: Pam Johnson. Front row: Sheila Morgan, -?-, Maureen Green, ? Danks, Christine Plant holding the ball and Joyce ?. *(Janet Armstrong Collection)*

Who are the key families in the development of Netherton? We try to identify some of them in the chapter on 'Netherton People' (page 65) and a walk among the tombs and graves in Netherton churchyard reveals a number of names. Here we see George Dunn (centre of back row) with his wife Ruth sitting below him. George Dunn was a coalmaster and well known public figure in the crucial late nineteenth-century period of Netherton's development. On the right are Mary (George's daughter) and her husband James Ernest Russell, proprietor of Swindell's Ironworks. On the left are Joseph and Fanny Russell (James's parents). On Mary Russell's lap is Dorothy Russell, the mother of Jean Wakeman who supplied the picture. *(Jean Wakeman)*

Can a twenty-first century Netherton be regenerated by the application of bricks and mortar? Can the planners save Netherton? If that seems fanciful, imagine the even greater difficulty of reinventing the quality of social life that was once experienced by a town like Netherton. At least the photographs show that it was possible once. Can Netherton, and similar Black Country townships, ever be more than just dormitories in the modern conurbation?

On a positive note, I must thank all those who have shared with me their enthusiasm for anything to do with Netherton. I am grateful for all the access I have been given to photograph collections and storehouses of knowledge and information. Often I hear people lament, 'But we never took photographs', but the amazing thing is that so many photographs have materialised, and hopefully it will do something to put Netherton on the record. Enjoy the collection and enjoy exploring Netherton.

Ned Williams, 2008

New generations of Nethertonians have learned about their local heritage via dance, drama, local history and community projects while in the local schools. Here, in 1983, pupils from Northfield Road School take part in a production with a local twist: *Aynuk Goes West*. *(School Archives)*

The park is one of Netherton's great assets, and has recently been the subject of improvements and home to the Netherton Fun Days. Here, in the early 1950s, we find members of the Primrose Hill League of Young Worshippers on the tennis courts: Colin Siviter, Doreen Walker, Margaret Shaw and Brian Owen. *(Brian and Hazel Owen)*

The Independent Order of Rechabites was a Friendly Society based on temperance principles, founded on 25 August 1835 in Salford. As it spread, the country was divided into districts, the 21st District being Birmingham. At a local level the branches were called 'Tents'. The Netherton Tent put this advert in the programme of the Wesleyan chapel's Autumn Bazaar of 1930. The Netherton Tent's secretary was G.F. Round, who owned a sweet and tobacco shop in Halesowen Road, and the leader was Fred H. Jennings, local entrepreneur and champion of the Wesleyan (Church Road) chapel.

There have been many attempts to cultivate Netherton's community spirit and sense of identity over the years. The production of *Netherton News* was a mid- to late 1980s attempt to wave the flag for Netherton. Recently the Friends of Netherton Park have worked hard and there have been many regeneration initiatives in the area. *(NW)*

Chapter One
The Main Drag

There are many approaches to Netherton and a variety of ways of crossing it, each providing a different way of experiencing the place. The most common way of seeing Netherton must be the journey along the old Dudley–Halesowen–Bromsgrove turnpike road, the A459. You may remember this as a journey on the 243 bus, or you may have present-day experiences of making a slow car journey along the same route. Today the Dudley Southern Bypass separates Dudley from Netherton and the driver can begin to feel he or she is entering Netherton at the moment of leaving the large island that marks the beginning of Cinder Bank. The latter climbs slightly and turns at it passes the site of Messiah Chapel and Netherton opens up ahead as a panorama. Passing the end of Swan Street, one is in a suburb of Netherton known as Baptist End. The next climb occupies part of the road once called High Street, the brow of which marks the gateway to Netherton's central district. From the hub of Netherton, the road, now calling itself Halesowen Road descends all the way down to the point where it crosses the Mousesweet Brook and passes into Old Hill.

Up until the end of the nineteenth century Pear Tree Lane turned northwards after passing the Windmill Works and crossed the railway line to join Blowers Green Road on the Dudley side of Shaw Road. This, at one time, must have been as close to Dudley as Netherton came. At some stage Pear Tree Lane was straightened and joined Cinder Bank on the Netherton side of the railway. This is where we now find Cinder Bank Island: the gateway to Netherton from the Dudley Southern Bypass. Since 1999 this statue has said 'Welcome to Netherton' to modern travellers. *(NW)*

Not the most beautiful of scenes, nevertheless, this view from the railway bridge at the foot of Blowers Green Road enables us to see the modified line of Pear Tree Lane as it passes Grazebrook's works. In the foreground is the GWR West Midland line heading towards Parkhead and all points south to Worcester. Blowers Green sidings signal-box was opened in 1916 and closed in early 1969. The railway, which in one way was a boundary between Dudley and Netherton at this point, remained open for freight until 1993 and now we wait to see if the Metro's rails will ever pass though this location, obscured as it is by the island on the bypass. *(Richard Taylor)*

A slight dip in the first stretch of Cinder Bank was occupied by an ungated railway level crossing where Grazebrook's private railway crossed the road. An 0–4–0ST, Grazebrook No. 2 (built by Peckett of Bristol in 1938) heads across Cinder Bank towards the exchange sidings close to Blowers Green Junction in the late 1950s. (See page 56 of *Netherton in Old Photographs*). *(Dudley Archives)*

Messiah Baptist Chapel was one of the first Netherton landmarks encountered on Cinder Bank travelling southwards, but the chapel was demolished soon after closure in 1979 and all that remains are the graves that once stood in front of it. The grave in the foreground can be identified in the picture of the chapel on page 125 of *Netherton in Old Photographs*. This 2006 picture shows us that the Heart of England Baptist Association still maintain the site. *(NW)*

The interior of Messiah Baptist Chapel during a service when the Round family, seen on the right, were taking part in the dedication of a chapel window, *c.* 1960. The three distinctive windows seen in the back of the picture matched windows at the other end that looked out over the graveyard. *(Margaret and Bernard Sylvester)*

Cinder Bank crests the bank at Messiah Chapel and then drops down past these houses to the junction with New Road, mid-1960s. Just beyond the lamppost is the building that was once the Jolly Collier public house. Coming towards the camera is Cinder Bank Castle (1887) and Fairview House (1890). On the left the pavement once provided a wonderful view looking down into the valley occupied by New Hall Farm, across the valley of the Black Brook and beyond towards Round Oak Steel Works. Today the road has been widened and the view is obscured by dense undergrowth. *(Dudley Archives)*

These terraces occupy the left-hand side of Cinder Bank between New Road and Swan Street, and seem to have been built in the 1890s. To the right can be seen the entrance to Jubilee Terrace, now blocked off (see page 15). Although shorn of their chimney pots and with some window modification, they have not changed significantly as can be seen in this 2005 photograph. On the right was Halls Joinery workshops and the terrace included Mrs Crispin's sweet shop and Dunn's fruiterers. *(NW)*

Looking along Cinder Bank towards the junction with Simms Lane in the mid-1960s. The left-hand side of the road was fully built up by the end of the nineteenth century and is the outer face of the area known as Baptist End (Swan Street, Prince Street, Round Street, etc.) Derelict colliery wasteland on the right was redeveloped later, and that side of the road is dominated by Corbett's Garage (see page 42 of *Netherton in Old Photographs*). The electric tramway built along this road in the early 1900s could be seen as having developed this area as a suburb of Dudley, but Baptist End was remarkably self-contained as sub-section of Netherton itself. *(Dudley Archives)*

Halfway along the terraced houses seen on the left of the upper picture there was a small turning (now blocked) which gave access to Jubilee Terrace, obviously built in 1897. Here we see Jubilee Terrace as renovated in 1980 by David Payne. These houses can now only be reached via Golding Street. *(Express & Star)*

Cinder Bank post office, sometimes known as Dudley Road, Netherton, although its address was 48 Cinder Bank. The first post-master was Edward Burchell, followed by his son Francis Victor. The latter's widow, Annie Burchell (1902–95) later took over, and ran the cake shop next door until that was leased to Mrs Phillips from Jubilee Terrace. The post office changed hands in the 1970s and then closed. *(Brian Burchell)*

Next to the post office were the cake shop and then the Hope Tavern on the corner of Swan Street, seen here in 2005. The phone box in the upper picture has been replaced with a modern box visible in this one. Note the Edwardian grandeur of the houses on the right, opposite the junction with Simms Lane. *(NW)*

Most people would associate the junction of Cinder Bank and Simms Lane with the firm of F.H. Jennings, auto-electrical engineers. Their premises have long been housed on this corner, having been first acquired by Fred H. Jennings in 1928. Although built as private dwellings the property had been swallowed up by the adjacent brewery. Fred H. Jennings moved in during 1930 after the first of many transformations. *(Jennings Collection)*

This view of two of Jennings' Morris vans looks back across Cinder Bank in the early 1960s. Fred H. Jennings became an Exide Batteries agent in 1922 and owned a number of well-decorated vans over the years. This picture also provides a glimpse of buildings on the other side of Cinder Bank, all of which survive today, but in changed ownership. (Both pictures supplied by the current owners of the business. *(Jennings Collection)*

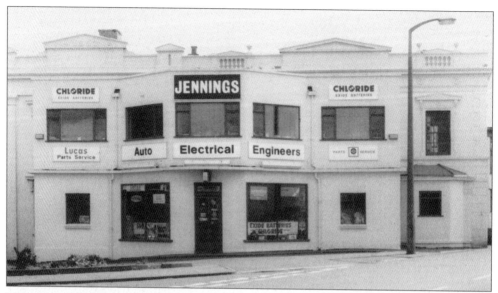

The Jennings building at the junction of Cinder Bank and Simms Lane as most of us will remember it. This picture was taken in 1978 and makes an interesting comparison with the picture on the previous page. In 2007 the frontage of the building was clad in metallic sheets and the appearance of the building changed again. *(Jennings Collection)*

This 2006 view of Cinder Bank looking across the road from the one-time Jennings premises seen on the previous page, prepares us for the task of placing the next two pictures. The house just behind the lamppost, no. 71, was formerly Garratt's shoe shop, but, of course, is now shorn of its distinctive window. The semis and the double-fronted house with the entry are nineteenth-century but the building on the far right was added later and began life as the original premises used by Fred Jennings. *(NW)*

Sixteen-year-old Ann Marie Boulger holds one of the Garratt children outside the family's shoe shop at 71 Cinder Bank, *c.* 1911. Ann Marie later married a Raybould, the famous milk retailers in old Netherton. *(Lindsey Cooper)*

Fred and Laurie Jennings stand on the left of this picture of the Jennings premises at 74 Cinder Bank. The story of Fred's purchase of this plot of land and the building of his home and retail premises is told elsewhere (see page 74), but this picture was taken some time after he had become an agent for Exide Batteries in 1922. The petrol pump did good trade until Corbett's opened their garage in Cinder Bank. *(Jennings Archive/Ann Clark)*

Right: Mary Jennings and the firm's van decorated for the 1924 Netherton carnival. This garage was also part of the premises at 74 Cinder Bank.

The Crown Inn was an old Plant's Brewery Victorian pub on the stretch of Cinder Bank between Simms Lane Junction and the junction with St Thomas Street. This early 1960s picture reminds us that Plant's Brewery was taken over by Ansells. *(Dudley Archives)*

The area behind the Crown was developed as Park Road, named after Netherton's new park of 1902. Looking across from Cinder Bank towards Park Road in this contemporary photograph we have a clear view of Hampton's shoe factory (now converted into apartments) and the tower blocks, Arley Court and Compton Court, in Swan Street. *(NW)*

Tom and Della Roberts' shop at 102 Cinder Bank was known to most people simply as Della's. They came to the left-hand part of this building in 1956. They had to refurbish the premises, which had once been a corn merchant. In about 1960 they took over the right-hand half of the building, which had formerly been Tromans' wet fish shop. It is now a Premier store. *(Tom and Della Roberts Collection)*

Tom and Della Roberts seen outside their Cinder Bank shop just before their retirement on 4 November 1985. Back in 1956 they had operated the shop simply as a greengrocers, but having built up the business they converted it into a supermarket while still living above the premises. Tom grew up in Hill Street, Netherton, and had once kept pigs in Eardley's Fold by Little's shoe factory. *(Tom and Della Roberts Collection)*

Dr McAviney's surgery occupies the centre of this picture looking back towards Dudley along the next stretch of Cinder Bank. The surgery was directly opposite Tom and Della Roberts' shop. The shops on the right can be seen on page 74 of *Netherton in Old Photographs*, and the houses on the left have now been demolished. There is not much traffic in this early 1960s picture. *(Dudley Archives)*

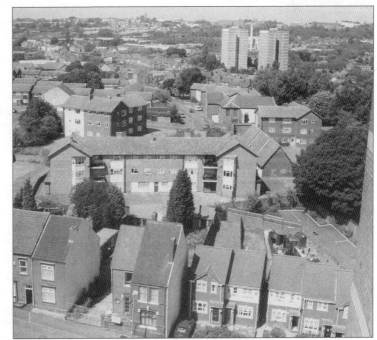

Looking back from the St John's Street flats towards Cinder Bank and beyond to the Swan Street flats and Top Church on the horizon in 2005. In the centre of the picture are the flats in Raybould's Fold, but behind them is the back of Sweet Turf Baptist Chapel nestling between St Giles' Street and Union Street. *(NW)*

The junction of High Street and Baptist End Road, 2006. The corner shop, now selling sandwiches, was used by the Grainger family for many years as a butcher's shop. Before that it had been Ashman's Bakery, and Effie Ashman ran a little sweet shop next door. The Ashmans lived behind the shop and they baked the bread in the building facing Baptist End Road. A couple of doors away in the High Street was C.H. Edwards, gentlemen's tailor. *(NW)*

This distinctive shop building occupies the corner of High Street and Arch Hill Street (the latter being added as an approach to the park after its opening in 1902), and Baptist End Road. After the war it was Harvey's Grocery (see pages 12 and 13 of *Netherton in Old Photographs*, in which Harvey's delivery van can be seen outside the shop). The café was renamed Katie's in September 1986, but has carried a variety of names since then. In the 1940s and '50s it was Capewell's electrical and radio stores. *(NW)*

The stretch of main road approaching the centre of Netherton was at one time called High Street but now Cinder Bank runs straight into Halesowen Road just before this point. Here are some High Street shops as they were in September 1986. *Above:* This pair of shops seems to belong to the Edwardian period of Netherton's development, after the building of Arch Hill Street and the opening of the park. Shops change very quickly but the types of business being carried on in both these shops has not changed in the last twenty years. The shop above was once occupied by Major Hipkiss, local painter and decorator turned builder. He was responsible for adding the second storey, and built his own house behind the shop facing Arch Hill Street.

Right: Denzil Hawkins, seen here in the doorway of his shop, no longer occupies these premises and they have become home to a gas service engineer rather than an electrician. *(NW)*

Once over the crest of the hill the main road becomes Halesowen Road and makes its way through the centre of Netherton, past the bank and the entrance to the park at the junction with Northfield Road. The triangle between Northfield Road and Halesowen Road can be seen beyond the zebra crossing, and this may once have been Netherton's market place (see pages 15 and 69 of *Netherton in Old Photographs*). The photograph is taken from Castle Street in the early 1960s.

This picture was taken at the same time facing in the other direction, looking towards Castle Street. The shops on the right at one time included the post office, Baker's general store and Clare Coley's dresswear shop. *(Dudley Archives)*

Looking across the old Market Place from the main road towards Northfield Road and the Public Hall, now known as Netherton Arts Centre, late 1940s or very early 1950s. Note the fire station and police houses (recently restored) next to the Public Hall in Northfield Road. The former tram pole in the foreground can also be seen in pictures on page 15 of *Netherton in Old Photographs*, but what is the mystery object behind the pole? Is it the drinking fountain from the junction with Cradley Road? *(Harry Rose)*

Looking back towards the bend that brings the main road into the centre of Netherton in the early 1960s. In the centre is the Castle public house, later replaced by the Malt Shovel which, in turn, has been replaced by housing. On the near side of St John's Street is Scrivens' Butchery shop (see page 6 of *Netherton in Old Photographs*). In recent years the busy bus stop has acquired its own lay-by. *(Dudley Archives)*

Another early 1960s picture taken from the corner of Cradley Road shows us the Swan Inn before its extension into the shop on the left, which was once Florrie Hamilton's pawn shop. Compare with the picture on page 78 of *Netherton in Old Photographs*. The George Mason store has become Skitt's, the estate agents. *(Dudley Archives)*

Between George Mason's store and Reeves' news agents was a menswear shop. In this picture the shop window is decorated to mark the Coronation of Elizabeth II in June 1953. *(Harry Rose)*

Above: The Dough Boy and Ruth's Knitting Shop once occupied the space above Allan's in Halesowen Road, but have both disappeared since this picture was taken in April 1986. *(NW)*

Right: It is difficult to realise that the Price's Rite Discount Store was once the smart menswear shop seen on the opposite page. This April 1986 picture also reveals that what had once been Reeves' newsagents was then operated by Messrs Jones & Kirton. The site of both buildings is now used by a Costcutter store. *(NW)*

An interesting view of the junction of Cradley Road and Halesowen Road in the centre of Netherton, 1907. Note the tram tracks and poles and the drinking fountain. The fountain is seen again on page 18 of *Netherton in Old Photographs*, but close inspection reveals that is not the same fountain that eventually appeared in the park. Beyond the Junction Inn (built in 1905) we catch a rare glimpse of the shops that were eventually replaced by the Labour Club, and beyond we can see the effect of subsidence on property in this area. *(Ken Rock)*

The shops built in 1908 to replace the buildings that had subsided along this stretch of the main road. Malcolm Cartwright came to the hairdressing shop in 1964, about the time this photograph was taken, and purchased the business in 1978. J.T. Smith's shop was sold to another cobbler and eventually Dr Gupta made it his surgery.

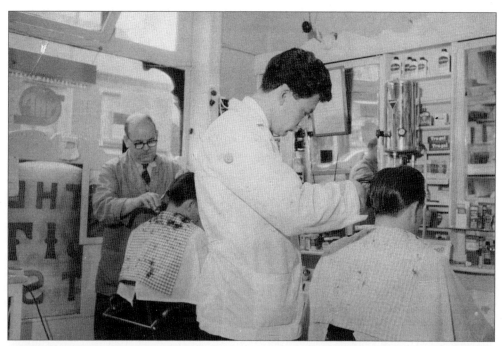

Inside the hairdressing shop at 82 Halesowen Road in the early 1960s. Once owned by Abner Walker, the shop was taken over by Vic Rushton, seen on the left, in about 1950. On the right is Vic's business partner, Mike Bradley. Malcolm Cartwright has owned the business since 1978 and supplied this picture and the one at the bottom of the previous page.

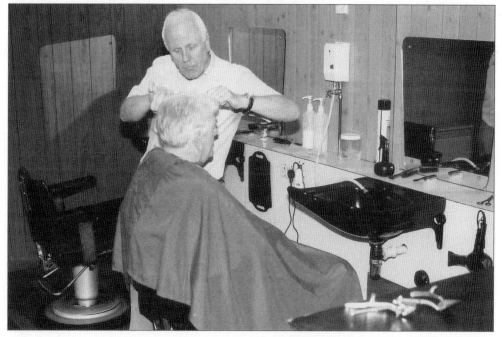

Malcolm Cartwright at work in his gents' hairdressing shop in 2006. The hand clippers in the foreground were used by Malcolm when he first came to shop in 1978. Since those times the interior and exterior of the premises have been considerably changed. (NW)

Malcolm Cartwright's shop as it looked in 2006, part of the block built in 1908, running from the 'new' façade of the Labour Club down to Mona's ladies hairdressing shop. Beyond we see a reminder of the subsidence problem and the premises that had once been Emile Doo's famous shop (see page 63 of *Netherton in Old Photographs*). *(NW)*

Returning to the other side of the road we come to Allan's. This part of his shop occupies the site of what was once Holden's shoe shop. Allan took over in the early 1970s and this picture was taken in the early 1980s. All the shops in the stretch are built on fairly long plots, providing Allan's with a cavernous interior. *(Allan Hodier)*

This picture was included to show that Allan's shop does indeed occasionally close! The main part of the shop on the left was Holden's shoe shop, which can be glimpsed in a picture on page 71 of *Netherton in Old Photographs*. The right-hand side was an electrical shop. Allan's shop has been on the site for over thirty years and this picture was taken in 2006. *(NW)*

Allan's shop with Allan at the till clutching a copy of *Netherton in Old Photographs*, April 2006. 'If we don't stock it, we'll try to get it', seems to be Allan's watchword. He also specialises in a large amount of seasonal goods ranging from Easter bunnies to Christmas lights. *(NW)*

Descending Halesowen Road from Allan's to Cross Street, 2005. The view above invites comparisons with the story forty years ago. The right-hand side of Allan's was an electrical shop; Roger Hills used to be J.L. Dunn's fruit and veg shop; Pizza Place was a branch of Marsh & Baxter's; China City was another fruit and veg shop; Panny's Plaice was Wimbush's cake shop; the empty shop was a haberdashery; Steve's Computers was a grocery shop, and Milan's chemist shop occupies the site of Bargain Basement. *(NW)*

By the early 1960s when this picture was taken Bargain Basement was reached by the pavement descending steps and the road passing by at a higher level. *(Dudley Archives)*

Another early 1960s view of Bargain Basement on Halesowen Road. This enables us to relate what is seen above to the situation below. The front windows of the building seen to the right of Bargain Basement in the above picture can be seen in the 1905 photograph below to show the effects of subsidence – walls crack and buildings sink. Presumably after this the road surface was raised and the premises on the left became a shop. *(Top: Dudley Archives; bottom: Mrs Hodgetts)*

A Red Diamond bus passes the site of Emile Doo's Pharmacy as it climbs towards central Netherton, June 2007. From here to Bishton's Bridge, in the far distance, the Halesowen Road was very prone to subsidence. Beyond the bus, on the left-hand side of the road were more shops, houses and a public house before reaching the Wakes Ground, which closed in 1966. A new health centre has been built on this stretch of the road. *(NW)*

Mihta and Mina Mahesh welcome the Mayor of Dudley, Cllr Tromans, to the Milan Chemist shop in 1991. Has he come to reassure them that subsidence in Netherton is now under control? The new shop occupies the former site of the Bargain Basement. *(Dot Tromans Collection)*

Looking back towards Cross Street we see Tilly Nott's veg shop in the background and Whittall's newsagents in the foreground, 1950s. Norman Whittall stands in the doorway of his family's shop as Grandad Whittall talks to Brenda Jones. Mrs Penn's drapery and millinery shop can just be seen on the far side of Cross Street. These buildings have now been demolished. *(Jack Phipps)*

Almost opposite Cross Street, the premises once used by Emile Doo, are now re-created at the Black Country Museum. Now in Halesowen Road the site is the home for Global Bathrooms, which also seem to be sinking below the level of the road. The extension to the building on the right became Whittall's newsagents when they vacated the premises seen in the picture above. *(NW)*

The Midland Red bus in the distance is just leaving the central shopping area of Netherton we have just looked at, and is heading down the long descent of the old turnpike road to Bishton's Bridge and then to Old Hill in the early 1960s. Some buildings seen here have now been demolished and the area occupied by the hoardings is now the site of a medical centre. *(Dudley Archives)*

From a high vantage point on the other side of the road, the photographer who took the picture above lets us see what was behind those hoardings. We see the extent of the old Netherton Wakes Ground – stretching across to Northfield Road. Pat Collins presented the fair on this ground from the turn of the nineteenth century up until the early 1960s, usually gaining access to the ground from Northfield Road. It has now been built upon. The hoardings occupy the site of demolished housing. *(Dudley Archives)*

An unusual view of this section of the Halesowen road at night with the entrance to Skan's petrol station in the foreground. The buildings in the background, including Tony's Café, have now been demolished. *(Janet Armstrong)*

Skan's Garage, June 1965. Pat Sly assists at the pumps in the days before self-service. Mr Skan Snr had to sell a Singer Gazelle to buy the lease on the petrol station from Mobil, but soon purchased the Morris van for the business. The Skans moved in during October 1964. *(Bob Skan Collection)*

Skan's Garage, the Netherton Service Station, on the Halesowen road. Mrs Hilda Skan, Joe ?, Bob Skan Jnr and friend David Sly pose beside the pumps in the late 1960s. At first Mr Skan Snr was the mechanic and Bob Jnr, assisted with sales and did the accounts, but it was very much a case of all the family and friends being involved. The Skan family left the business in the mid-1980s and the site is now devoted to car sales. *(Bob Skan Collection)*

The site was quite run down when the Skan family moved in, but it became a smart, busy petrol station over the twenty years they were in charge. They had to deal with the introduction of Green Shield Stamps, decimalisation and self-service, as well as the improvement and extension of the premises. Who remembers queueing for petrol before a public holiday and filling up with four gallons for less than a pound? *(Bob Skan Collection)*

The junction of Northcott Street and the Halesowen road in the early 1960s. Northcott Road was previously called North Street, and together with Chapel Street and Washington Street, comprised the suburb of Primrose Hill, an area cleared of much of its housing in the late 1940s. The demolition site on the extreme left appears again in the next picture. *(Dudley Archives)*

The three-bedroom semis built along the Halesowen Road conceal a history of intense coal-mining in the area, although dips in the road remind us of the subsidence it caused. On page 19 of *Netherton in Old Photographs* is an earlier view looking across to this stretch of road when Dudley Wood Colliery pit no. 2 occupied the land on which these houses were built. This picture was taken in the early 1960s. *(Dudley Archives)*

Opposite the streets of Primrose Hill was the entrance to Netherton Goods station and the canal interchange facilities at Withymoor Basin. This was the terminus of the goods-only branch of the GWR from Windmill End Junction just south of Baptist End which was opened in 1879 and closed in 1965. The tug on the left is just pulling its trailer out of Washington Street – home to Hingley's Netherton Ironworks. *(Dudley Archives)*

The crane seen beside the parked car in the top picture now appears on the right of this picture as we look back towards the Halesowen Road, but such is the angle we see Danks' works across the background of the picture rather than Hingley's on the far side of the road. The track past the offices of Netherton Goods station continued right across to Northfield Road but was not really a public right of way. We catch a glimpse of the interior of the transshipment shed on the left, early 1960s. *(Dudley Archives)*

Descending from Bishton's Bridge, the Halesowen road comes to a busy crossroads. Cole Street crosses the main road to become Saltwells Road and at one time the corrugated iron school seen above dominated the scene. The 'Iron Schools' had opened in 1885 and lasted until 1962 when it was officially called Halesowen Road Secondary School. *(Dudley Archives)*

When the 'Iron Schools' were demolished they were replaced by prefabricated buildings of a more modern type. These became Saltwells First School, which opened in 1964 with a life expectancy of ten years. In the end it lasted twice that long – finally closing in 1984 soon after this picture was taken. Saltwells First had a much-used swimming pool and transferring the pupils to what became Netherbrook School was not a very popular move. Today an Aldi supermarket and car park occupies the site. *(Clarice Walters Collection)*

The present-day view from Bishton's Bridge looks past the Canal Walk development of new apartments, over the Saltwells Road crossroads and down the Halesowen Road towards the boundary, passing the Lidl supermarket and the Moot Meet public house on the left. Bishton was a canal carrier who operated a packet boat service from here to Birmingham after the opening of the Netherton tunnel. *(NW)*

Travel West Midlands bus no. 598 on the 243 service passes the Moot Meet public house, 1 August 2007. The pub opened in May 1957 and the name refers to its proximity to the boundary at the Mousesweet Brook, which the bus has just crossed. Representatives of the Moots of the two shires on either side of the brook met in the area to discuss boundary disputes in medieval times. Unfortunately a good picture of a Midland Red bus passing through Netherton on the 243 service has yet to be found. *(NW)*

Chapter Two
Exploring the Side Streets

The old character of Netherton is still preserved in some of its side streets, despite massive programmes of demolition that began in the 1950s and continue to the present day. Old streets can still be found bearing names like 'fold' and 'row', although they maybe now be filled with modern housing, or no houses at all. There are passages with names like 'The Six Foot' and 'The White Bricks', and there is confusion arising from many streets being renamed to distinguish them from roads in Dudley with the same name. In the mid-nineteenth century when the Road Board was laying out some of the streets of Netherton there was an obsession with saintliness: St Giles, St Thomas, St George, St James and, of course, St Andrew. This chapter looks at St John's Street as a representative of Netherton's side streets, each one almost a self-contained community. It then doubles back via Hampton Street to show the nineteenth-century survivors and provides a glimpse of places like North Street where post-war demolition has left nothing but memories and very few photographs.

Cinder Bank runs through the centre of this view from Compton Court, but is fairly hidden from view. The Conservative Club and its bowling green, and Hillcrest School help the reader to get their bearings, but above all the picture provides a glimpse of how Netherton consists of a number of slightly separate networks of side streets. This side of Cinder Bank is home to streets around Park Road, and the far side climbs the hill from the Sweet Turf area up towards St John's Street, etc. The tower of St Andrew's peeps above the trees. *(NW)*

In April 1986 Win's the greengrocers on the corner of St John's Street, was still using the little warehouse behind the shop. The building was demolished rather suddenly in February 2007 just as some people were hoping it might be restored and preserved. It had originally been a hay, straw and grain store used by the Cole family. John Cole (1819–83) had been a butcher at 1 St John Street and his descendent, Florence Cole, was still living there until her disappearance in 1999. Planned development of the site is sympathetic to the proportions and textures of the Cole family buildings. *(NW)*

Now the little warehouse has been demolished we have a clear view of the Sunday School building behind St John's (New Connexion) Methodist Chapel. The Sunday School is thought to be older than the chapel, which dates from 1848, with a new frontage added in 1898. The Methodists left at the end of 1990 and it is now a Pentecostal Church. *(NW)*

St John's Methodist Chapel appears on the right of this picture as we take in a view of the other side of St John's Street in the mid-1960s. The empty ground in the foreground had once been occupied by Meeting Street, Griffin's Row and Victoria Street, but is now occupied by high-rise flats. The Miners Arms forms the centrepiece of the picture. *(Dudley Archives)*

The exterior of the Miners Arms, St John's Street, is illustrated on page 88 of *Netherton in Old Photographs*. Here we go inside to meet Kath and Jim Pugh behind the bar in about 1960. They had moved to the pub in 1958 and Jim worked there until his death in 1969. Kath carried on until the age of sixty in 1981. After that date the pub closed and has since become offices. *(Kath Taylor)*

The WVS delivering meals on wheels in St John's Street, August 1961. The picture gives us a view of the other side of the road, opposite the Miners Arms, and we can see the high-side pavement and the houses that have been cleared in the photograph on page 47. The 'barrier' can still be seen in that picture although the houses have gone! *(NW)*

The Bulls Head, seen here in 2005, carries the street name Netherton Hill. Although it now seems to be in St John's Street, there were originally houses built in front of it and Netherton Hill was reached via Harris's Fold, seen on the left. *(NW)*

From just above the Bull this passage leads across to Church Road from St John's Street. It was universally known as 'The Six Foot'. Amazingly it survives although often rather overgrown and very much overshadowed by the modern blocks of flats. *(Brian Payton Collection)*

At the point where St John's Street crosses St Andrew's Street, we come face to face with the Five Ways public house. St John's Street continues on the right of the pub. Behind the pub was Five Ways Brewery, opened in about 1835 but expanded when it was taken over by John Rolinson in 1877. His son Daniel continued the business and bought further properties as well as becoming a Dudley councillor. The brewery closed in 1925 and the pubs were taken over by Wolverhampton & Dudley Breweries. *(NW)*

Above: The upper portion of St John's Street is nicely displayed in these two early 1960s pictures. Bell Road can be seen joining St John's Street on the right and the off-licence on the corner was licensed to Edith Florence Grainger in the 1960s. The corner shop on the left reappears in the centre of the picture below – a reminder that there were many shops in St John's Street. *Below:* The very top of the street where it runs into Hill Street. *(Dudley Archives)*

A few yards away was Hampton Street and another brewery! This 2007 view looks up Hampton Street, across Hill Street and into Crescent Road. This handsome building was once Ike's Shop. Once across Bell Road (behind the camera) it was once possible to walk 'The White Bricks' – another famous Netherton byway – to reach King Street. The whole area reflects the expansion of Netherton between 1865 and the turn of the twentieth century. *(NW)*

In central Netherton some nineteenth-century housing has survived, but in the Primrose Hill area houses in Chapel Street and North Street were demolished in slum clearance that began in 1964. Some people ventured into their back yards to take pictures that would provide a record of the area. Winifred Collie was photographed at the back of 55 Chapel Street about sixty years ago. *(Sheila Round)*

Almost next door to Hampton Street and King Street was Hill House, which faced Church Road. It was the home of James Ernest Russell and his wife Jane. He was the proprietor of Swindell's, and Jane was the daughter of George Dunn (see page 8). In Edwardian Netherton masters and men lived in close proximity. *(Jean Wakeman)*

Church Road provides endless fascination, obviously planned to connect the parish church to the centre of its community, but slow to develop east of St Andrew's Street. This picture was taken in 1938 when the wilderness of the Yew Tree Hills came right down to the south side of Church Road. The house on the right, on the corner of Bell Road, was once a manse and can still be admired today. To the left of the picture large houses were well set back from Church Road – walls and gateways survive to indicate the size of their plots. Hill House, of the same ilk, was just to the right of this picture. *(Dudley Archives)*

Chapter Three

Transport

All forms of transport played their part in the development of Netherton from the construction of the Dudley–Halesowen–Bromsgrove turnpike road through the era of canal construction, followed by railway building, and back to the importance of roads.

The canal system, when at its peak, almost turned Netherton into an island – joined to the rest of Britain by Cinder Bank. The construction of the Netherton canal tunnel in the 1850s put Netherton on the canal map at a time when most people were thinking about railways, but then railways never came very directly to Netherton as far as passenger traffic was concerned. The Netherton Goods Branch of 1879, however, provided a freight-carrying service to the heart of Netherton and provided important interchange with the canal.

The electric street tramway reached Netherton in 1900, which was an important point in the development of Netherton's growing confidence in itself as an urban community. Road transport has reigned supreme ever since.

One of Netherton's well-known canal locations is the Sounding Bridge, seen in this postcard view from the opposite side of the bridge to the picture on page 26 of *Netherton in Old Photographs*. The Dudley No. 2 Canal turns away from the valley of the Blackbrook at this point and begins to circle the Yew Tree Hills to make its way round Netherton. The canal opened in May 1798, but in 1838 this particular stretch was created by re-alignment and the building of the Lodge Farm Reservoir. The re-aligned stretch incorporated a short tunnel called Brewin's Tunnel. This was later opened out as a cutting, and the bridge installed in 1858. The canal worker's cottage, seen in the picture, stands between the canal and a corner of the reservoir and is still there today. (*Megan Crofts*)

The Netherton Canal Tunnel is another well-known canal location in the area. Here the tunnel approach is being used for moorings at a National Waterways Association rally in 1996. See also the picture on page 38 of *Netherton in Old Photographs*. The Netherton Tunnel was opened in August 1858 and gave access from the area served by the Dudley No. 2 Canal (Netherton, Old Hill, Halesowen, etc.) to the main line of the Birmingham Canal Navigation at the other end of the tunnel. *(Terry Alliband)*

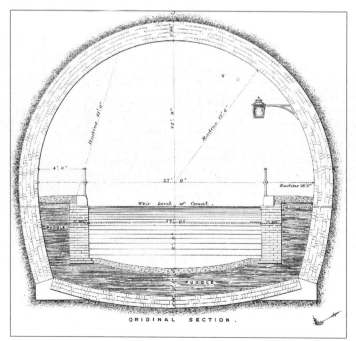

The Netherton Tunnel was always likely to face problems with subsidence. This drawing of a cross-section of the tunnel, by C.H. Nias, was made in 1902 when the tunnel closed for nine weeks while a subsidence problem was resolved. Mr Nias was the resident engineer in charge of the work. A total of 63 yds of the canal had to be rescued, and the work proceeded twenty-four hours a day to put matters right. *(Keith Hodgkins)*

Above: A view from the St Peter's Road bridge at the 1991 National Waterways Festival in Netherton, looking towards the tunnel with Cobb's Engine House visible in the distance. The branch to the left is the former main line, now a short spur to the boatyard. *(Terry Alliband)*
Below: Looking back towards Northfield Road. *(Doris Corbett)*

The railway that came closest to serving Netherton was the line from Dudley (Blowers Green Junction) to Old Hill, known locally as the Bumble Hole Line, opened in 1878. Here we see ex-GWR Prairie tank 2–6–2T no. 4147 hauling a train up the bank from Baptist End to Blowers Green Junction. Behind the smoke of the banker we can see New Road, and on the right are the premises of the Staffordshire Wagon Repair Company, 10 August 1965. *(Richard Taylor)*

The view from New Road looking south, 3 July 1965. Ex-GWR Prairie tank 2–6–2T no. 6129 had become derailed and ex-LMS Stanier 2–8–0 no. 48516 has brought in the breakdown crane to lift the engine back onto the track, while a growing crowd turns out to watch. In the background is the site of Big K, a pioneering DIY store. The track at this point is now a footpath. *(David Willetts)*

A trackside view of ex-GWR 2–6–2T no. 6129 being lifted back onto the rails between Baptist End and Blowers Green Junction on 3 July 1965. The railway closed to passenger traffic on 13 June 1964 and to freight traffic officially on 1 January 1968, but that was postponed for a few months. *(David Willetts)*

The Old Hill-bound railcar in the distance has just passed Windmill End Junction and its signal-box in this picture taken from the end of the platform at Baptist End Halt, May 1963. The signalman's duties included tending the lamps on the impressive junction signal seen on the right. *(David Wilson)*

Two photographs taken on 23 September 1956 at Windmill End. Sometimes the Bumble Hole
Line was used for through trains diverted from their normal route, or for excursion trains. A
double-headed train approaches Windmill End in the top picture showing interesting features
of the canal landscape, and leaves Windmill End in the picture below, showing the station
footpath, and new housing in the village. In the bottom picture the old wooden footbridge
can be seen and the wooden buildings, partly demolished, in anticipation of modernising the
line. *(Mike Hughes)*

The diesel bubble-car heads for Old Hill through Windmill End Halt just before the closure of the line in June 1964. Corrugated iron shelters, like the one on the left, were provided at all the halts, plus new concrete platforms, during the 1950s. The rather more elaborate shelter on the right must have been recognition of Windmill End's former status as a station rather than a halt. *(NW)*

Darby End Halt (seen here), Baptist End Halt and Old Hill (High Street) Halt were all added to the line in 1905. They originally had wooden platforms and iron shelters but the style shown here was the result of the mid-1950s modernisation. Ex-GWR 0–6–0PT No. 6403 runs into Darby End Halt in the early 1960s. The location of the halt is more clearly seen on page 30 of *Netherton in Old Photographs*, but is difficult to imagine now as nearly all traces of the line at this point have been obliterated. *(John Dew)*

The Netherton Goods branch opened in 1879, one year after the Dudley–Old Hill line, from which it diverged at Windmill End Junction. 0–6–0PT no. 9614 is seen on the branch in these early 1960s pictures. *Above:* The engine and brake van wait to return to the junction on the stretch between Northfield Road and the Greaves Road Bridge. *Below:* We look back across the Northfield Road level crossing into the yard. Further pictures of the yard itself appear on page 42. *(Richard Taylor)*

Right: Amazingly, the Greaves Road bridge survives today, despite never seeming to have served any purpose! The trackbed is now a footpath. *(NW)*

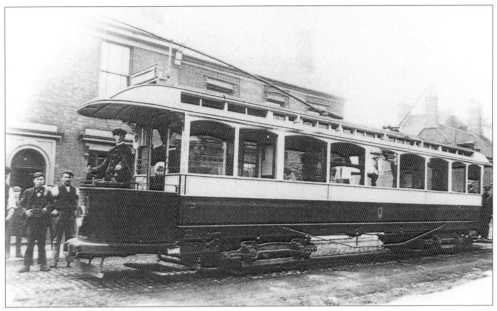

Good pictures of road transport in Netherton seem rarer than rail pictures. The Dudley, Stourbridge & District Electric Traction Company was a subsidiary of the British Electric Traction group, and opened the line from Dudley to Cradley Heath, via Netherton and Old Hill on 5 October 1900. *Above:* A Cradley Bogie car, built by the Brush Co., was photographed in Cradley Heath with driver Baker at the controls. *(Squire Baker)*

A very touched-up picture survives of Netherton's last tram (or perhaps simply a tram photographed on the last day of service). Trams between Dudley and Cradley Heath, via Netherton, were withdrawn on 31 December 1929, and were replaced by Midland Red buses. Driver Howard Whitehouse and conductor Victor John Skidmore pose by a standard Tividale tramcar of the type preserved at the Black Country Museum. *(P.J. Edwards)*

An Albion canvas-roofed coach (not really a charabanc) was part of the fleet of coaches built up by Holdens – first in Cradley Road, and then in Baptist End Road. This photograph was supplied by the son of the man standing behind the door wearing the button-hole. *(Dom Kirby)*

Buses belonging to Black Country Tours parked in Northfield Road outside the garage and portacabin head office of the company early in 2006. Buses of the fleet are a familiar sight all over the Black Country and have carried names of Black Country legends like Dolly Allen and Aynuk and Ayli. The garage in the background was at one time used by Davenports Coaches. *(NW)*

Bissell's owned businesses on both sides of the Halesowen road on the stretch between the town centre and Bishton's Bridge, ranging from brush manufacture to timber and fuel supplies. Here we see examples of horse-drawn and motor transport used by the firm. *(John Shaw)*

One of the many vans used by Fred H. Jennings of Cinder Bank. *(Ann Clark)*

Local industry created a demand for heavy haulage and here we see a Scammell tractor unit, belonging to Wynn's Transport, picking up a pressure vessel from Thompson's works in Pear Tree Lane, *c.* 1970. It is seen here leaving the new shop where all the biggest jobs were completed. *(Mike Woodall)*

A Scammell Highwayman tractor unit belonging to Pickfords is seen climbing the Halesowen road towards Bishton's Bridge in the mid-1960s with a load from Stewart & Lloyds works at Coombes Wood. Note the man on the load with the pole who will lift sagging phone wires as the load passes through Netherton. *(Roger Mills)*

Chapter Four
The People of Netherton

This chapter brings together a selection of Nethertonians, some dealt with individually and some portrayed as members of the groups to which they belong. Such a collection can never be comprehensive, but hopefully it will seem representative. We begin by looking at some of the founding fathers who fought on Netherton's behalf on Dudley Council; continue via some Nethertonians who became Mayor of Dudley and then delve in the many diverse activities of Nethertonians in general.

Netherton carnival, 1930. Cousins Joan Hipkiss and Betty Doo attend the Carnival Queen, Miss Nellie Bloomer. The 'King of Mirth' was Alf Carter and the jester was Cyril Stanley. Maids of honour were Florrie and Gladys Bannister, Irene Shaw and Susan Walker. *(Betty Spooner Collection, via Rob and Meg Grainger)*

George Henry Dunn was born in Netherton on 23 September 1837, in a small cottage within half a mile of his eventual home at Netherton House. He started work in a local colliery at the age of eleven, earning 6d a day. He literally worked his way from the bottom up, learning everything there was to know about fetching coal. When he eventually became an employer for the first time in 1868, he lost no opportunity in improving the conditions for his men. He became a coalmaster, leasing the rights to mine coal in Netherton Collieries from the Earl of Dudley.

He began life as a New Connexion Methodist, but later defected to the Church of England. Interestingly, he was a loyal member of the congregation of St Andrew's Church but never sought any office. Politically he started out as a Liberal, but he left them in 1885 to become a Conservative, but he remained very much a man of independent mind rather than party politician. His passion was self-improvement and the improvement of his community. He first joined Dudley Council in 1874 when elected unopposed to represent Netherton.

He was interested in everything from mines drainage and sewage disposal, to education and culture. He joined the School Board in 1892 and then became Chairman of the Education Committee when education was municipalised in 1902. In November 1897 he was made Mayor of Dudley and served two terms. While mayor he laid the foundation stone of Dudley Opera House, and during his second year of office he was made an alderman.

Dunn played a major part in developing Netherton and its infrastructure. He was keen to see electricity and electric trams brought to Netherton. He supported the building of the Public Hall and library and played his part in seeing the old colliery wastes turned into the Recreation Ground. He was a magistrate and a Governor of Birmingham University, a Freemason and supporter of local friendly societies – the list is endless! To mark his seventieth birthday a banquet was held in his honour on 23 September 1907, and the following year his portrait was commissioned and placed in the local collection.

He died on 20 July 1908 at his home in Netherton House in Hall Street, between Simms Lane and Cinder Bank. The building is now the Conservative Club. His funeral was a major event and he was buried in the family vault in Netherton Churchyard. His colleague, Cllr James Smellie said, 'The late Alderman was brusque in his manner, most dogmatic and pugnacious, and yet he never bore malice and was possessed of a very tender heart. His grasp of details, his marvellous memory, his unerring accuracy and his love of work gave him a power and influence he could not otherwise have achieved.'

Barney Norton
(1876–1933).
(*Megan Crofts*)

Barney Norton was born forty years after George Dunn and was part of that later generation of public figures whose development began in nineteenth-century Liberalism, but who gradually made their way into the emerging Labour Party of the twentieth century.

He worked at Noah Hingley's in the puddling and forging department and eventually became Secretary of the Puddlers & Forgemen's Union. Like many workers at Hingley's, he lived close to the works, in Chapel Street, Primrose Hill. He was a founder member of Netherton Labour Club and was its first president. He was first elected to Dudley Council in 1919 but lost his seat in 1922.

He returned in 1926 and served on a number of committees, displaying great interest in the work of the Public Assistance Committee. He was regarded as a straight-to-the-point kind of local politician rather than a great orator.

He died on 31 July 1933 as a result of a seizure while in Netherton Labour Club. The *Dudley Herald* told its readers, 'The working classes of Dudley have lost a sincere friend and outspoken champion.' On 4 August he was buried in Netherton Churchyard, after a funeral service conducted at Primrose Hill Congregational Church.

Henry Joseph Golding grew up in a Netherton family. His uncle, James Golding, was the first headmaster of Dudley Upper Standard School – which much later became the Gilbert Claughton School at Blowers Green. His grandfather was the Joseph Golding who had established a local building firm, which in turn passed to Henry's father. Henry began his working life at a carpenter's bench in the family business.

Like Barney Norton, he was born in Netherton in the 1870s but came from a more middle-class background. He was a life-long member of the congregation of St Andrew's Church and held various offices in connection with it. He was also an unwavering Conservative but enjoyed good relations with people drawn from all sections of the community. His first act of public service was to join the Board of Guardians in 1917. In 1922 Nethertonians elected him to Dudley Council.

The year 1933 saw the death of Dudley's Mayor, Alderman Fullwood, and Alderman Golding was asked to take on the role. He was very aware of current levels of unemployment, and one of his first acts as mayor was to reinvigorate the Mayor's Boots & Clothing Fund. During August 1933 Henry Golding was taking a holiday at Rhos-on-Sea, North Wales, when he was taken unwell and sought the advice of a doctor. He died at the doctor's surgery on Sunday 27 August 1933 and the news had to be relayed to Dudley and Netherton that the town had lost two mayors in less than a year.

His funeral was held in Netherton the following Thursday and crowds lined the streets as the cortège made its way from Henry Golding's home in Church Road up to Netherton Church. Such was his popularity with all sections of society that the number of mourners was vast. Every society and institution was well represented.

The *Dudley Herald* told readers, 'He was one of those men whose character has a certain unostentatious beauty, that hidden something which cannot help but attract the admiration of everybody. He was ever seeking to promote the wellbeing of his native ward – Netherton – where he had many friends.'

Henry Golding Snr (1840–1914). As explained above, Joseph Henry Golding eventually ran the Netherton-based building contracting firm started by his grandfather, Joseph Golding. Joseph had taken his son, Henry, on as partner, and in turn Henry took on his own son in the early 1900s.Henry Golding Snr had never taken any part in public life, but like his son was a keen supporter of St Andrew's Church. He sang in the choir for forty years. His wife was the daughter of Cllr Round, another early champion of Netherton. He died on 13 March 1914 at his home, Westlands and is buried in Netherton churchyard.

John Walter Barnsley of Primrose House was born in Netherton on 28 January 1855, but left the town to be educated. For a short time it looked as if he might make education his career and he became headmaster of the Clearwell School in the Wye Valley. However in the early 1880s he was recalled to Netherton to join his father's firm. He became the company chairman and became deeply involved in Netherton life.

He was president of the Netherton Conservative Club for twenty-five years and was an active member of Netherton Cricket Club. He became a magistrate but did not seek election to the council. Like the Goldings, he was associated with St Andrew's Church. He died on 31 May 1934 in his office, and is buried in Netherton churchyard. He married twice and, as is so often the case, the famous names of Netherton inter-married. One of John Barnsley's daughters, for example, married Harold Emile Doo, the famous chemist.

John Walter Barnsley (1855–1934). *(Betty Doo Collection)*

William and Rose Wakeman

William Wakeman was born on 12 October 1900 in a little cottage in Baptist End Lane. At the age of fifteen he joined the Great Western Railway as a clerk at Hockley. He eventually became stationmaster at Windmill End in 1938, where he stayed until moving to Blowers Green in August 1943. He retired from the railway about 1962, having enjoyed a forty-five years' service presentation in 1960.

William married Rose Wyer on 27 December 1920, and in 1929 they moved to an almost new council house at 45 Walker Street. Both of them were interested in local politics, and William was first elected to represent Castle Ward in 1933. He left the council during the war years and returned to represent Netherton in 1945. He became Mayor of Dudley in May 1955, with Rose as his mayoress. Rose herself also served on Dudley Council as an Independent, whereas William was a member of the Labour Party. Rose was first elected to the council in 1956, while acting as mayoress. She was also a magistrate from 1956 until 1970.

William died on 12 August 1988, having been involved in the local community all his life. He appears on page 81 of *Netherton in Old Photographs* among fellow members of the Ancient Order of Buffaloes. It is surprising to think that he was the first Mayor of Dudley to come from Netherton since the days of Henry Golding.

William Wakeman in his role as station master at Windmill End, with porter Jimmy Male in 1939. *(Author's Collection)*

Alderman Wakeman in his mayoral robes,
1955. *(Wakeman Collection)*

The official portrait of Dudley's Mayor and Mayoress, William and Rose Wakeman, 1955.
(Bert Bissell Collection)

Mayor Wakeman's Civic Sunday procession in Chapel Street, making its way to Primrose Hill Chapel, June 1955. They are accompanied by the town clerk, Mr Wadsworth, the Recorder and Mayor's Chaplain, the Revd Mr Swanbury. *(Wakeman Collection)*

Rose Wakeman and Mayor Sam Danks look on as William Wakeman, in his role as an alderman, meets Queen Elizabeth II at Dudley Town Hall, 23 April 1957. *(Wakeman Collection)*

Cllr Geoff Tromans was Mayor of Dudley
from May 1991 to May 1992. Geoff was
born on 9 July 1927 and joined the council
in 1978. He served on the council until
his death on 17 February 2000. He was
born in the White City in Quarry Bank but
became a Nethertonian as a result of his
marriage. He and and his wife Dot
moved into a house in Cope Road.
(Dot Tromans Collection)

Cllr Geoff Tromans looks on as Mrs Rose Cook from Primrose Road shakes hands with Tony
Boden, Area Contracts Manager for Tarmac, to mark the completion of the modernisation
of 151 council properties on the Yew Tree Hills. They are also watched by local residents
Gill and Cliff Cooper, and the location is the Netherton Estates Office in Church Road.
(Dot Tromans Collection)

Joe Billingham was born in 1904 and joined the Labour Party in his late teens. He was first elected to Dudley Council in 1946 and became mayor in 1957 – the third Nethertonian in succession to be Mayor of Dudley. Here is seen here in his capacity as forgeman in the stamping department at Burton Delingpole Ltd of Old Hill. He was a man of many parts: he had played football for Woodside Wanderers, was interested in homing pigeons, was a chorister at St John's Church, Dudley Wood, and was a good Black Country dialect comedian who had been the 'King of Mirth' in Netherton's first carnival! *(W. Boyd)*

Mark Washington Fletcher was descended from the English branch of George Washington's family, and was born in 1882. His grandfather, William Washington, built a public house at Primrose Hill, Halesowen Road – The Loyal Washington. He became a magistrate in 1920, moving to the licensing bench in 1927. He chaired that committee for twenty-five years. He was a Labour councillor from 1927 to 1938, and was re-elected as a Conservative in 1939. In 1948 he wrote history of Netherton called *From Edward to Edward. (Erena Little)*

Mark Washington Fletcher.
(A portrait by John Little, of Dudley Photographic Society and Netherton's famous shoe factory. 1965.)

Joe Darby, born at Darby End on 6 August
1861, became arguably Netherton's most famous
son. From an early age he displayed remarkable
aptitude for jumping – a branch of athletics in
which he made his name.

He appeared before the Prince of Wales
(later Edward VII) on 10 November 1888. It was
in the late 1880s that he was at his peak, and
made several extensive foreign tours to display
his skills. When he returned to Dudley on 12
July 1889 he was given a full civic welcome and
presented with a championship belt, which is now
preserved in Dudley Museum.

His amazing jumps broke world records and
were performed for entertainment as well as sport.
For example, in January 1898 he was appearing
in Tony Felix's show in a circus building just off
Hall Street in Dudley. After his jumping career was
over he became publican at the Albion Tavern in
Dudley, and died at the end of 1937.

The Revd Canon Samuel James Marriott was the minister at St Andrew's Church,
Netherton, for forty-five years, and was well known throughout Dudley, as well as in
Netherton. He was a native of Northamptonshire. He was ordained as a deacon in 1874
in the same year that he gained his degree and then proceeded to gain his MA and be
ordained as a priest. By this time he had come to Dudley and was a curate attached to St
Thomas's Church.

He was sent to St Andrew's, Netherton, in 1878, and began his long and successful
ministry in which congregation grew in number, and the fabric of the church building was
enhanced. From the vast vicarage he organised garden parties and tennis tournaments, and

became a member of Netherton Cricket Club.
The social activities at the vicarage raised vast
sums of money for church restoration and
improvements.

The Revd Mr Marriott was a highly educated
man and some thought he could have delivered
his rather literary sermons in Latin as easily
as in English, but that did not prevent him
mixing with all walks of life in his industrial
parish. He served on countless committees
concerned with educational, religious and
social matters. Marriott died in January 1923
at the age of seventy-eight and the parishioners
placed a stained-glass window in his memory
among the northside windows. He had placed
a window here in memory of his wife when the
church had been refurbished in 1903. A huge
funeral was followed by his burial in Netherton
churchyard.

Fred H. Jennings was born on 31 October 1881 – Wake Monday – in a house near Simms Lane. He left school at thirteen and undertook a variety of jobs. He even tried working for himself as a painter and decorator. New opportunities arose when working for Hingley's and Fred pursued the study of chemistry and electrical engineering to aid his progress at the firm. One day he was blinded in one eye while at work, and suffered various other setbacks. He eventually deciding to leave Hingley's and start up his own business.

In 1914 he purchased land in Cinder Bank and started building the house, which became no. 74. He and his family moved in during 1915. Fred ran an electrical installation business from 74 Cinder Bank and also worked as a projectionist for Mr Bishop at the Public Hall during the evenings. Between them Fred and his wife, Jennie, also ran an electrical retailing business from the shop on the ground floor of no. 74. As the end of the war approached, Fred had installed a petrol pump on the premises and was moving into auto-electrical engineering. By 1922 he had become an agent for Exide batteries and the famous Fred H. Jennings business was born.

Fred was also a very committed Methodist and an active member of the Rechabites. He was something of a workaholic and led a life of many strands – most of which he recalled in a memoir written late in life, and some of which found its way into a privately printed history of the business. The photograph shows Fred standing outside his garage/workshop at the home he acquired in Marriott Road. The house, now a dentist's surgery, housed the Jennings Family from 4 November 1933 onwards, and later other properties were built

or acquired close by to create quite an enclave of Jenningses!

Fred H. Jennings bought land in Marriott Road in 1929 and eventually built this house in 1933. He lived there for the rest of his life and died on 26 October 1964 – a week short of his 83rd birthday. It is now a dental surgery. *(NW)*

Fred H. Jennings stands with his hands in his pockets outside the premises he had built at 74 Cinder Bank. It was built by William Tilley and cost £300. Fred was able to move into the building in March 1915 (see picture on page 20). Standing next to the vehicle is Laurie Jennings, Fred's brother, who joined the business in about 1920. This picture appears to date from about 1925. *(Ann Clark)*

Stanley Jennings, seen on the left, was born in 1908, and joined his father's business about 1926. Stanley and his brother Wesley Jennings later became directors in the company registered by their father back in 1929. This picture was taken in 1981 when the firm became agents for Radiomobile products. *(Ann Clark)*

Betty Doo was born in 1923, and died on 25 January 2007, aged eighty-four. She was 100 per cent Netherton and never lost her interest in the community in which she lived. Betty was the daughter of Harold Emile Doo (known as Jack) and Katherene Barnsley, known as Rene (see pages 63 and 64 of *Netherton in Old Photographs*). After attending Dudley Girls' High School, Betty became a metallurgist with Accles & Pollack, and later a member of staff at Wednesbury Technical College. She had a life-long association with St Andrew's Church and with the cultural life of Netherton, particularly via amateur dramatics. Betty was buried in the Barnsley family vault in Netherton churchyard.

Betty Doo as a child and as a young woman. *(Meg and Rob Grainger Collection)*

Drama has been a feature of the lives of the schools and churches of Netherton, and the Netherton Arts Centre has been the home of Dudley Little Theatre for many years. Here we see this tradition represented by the cast of John Drinkwater's *A Man's House*, performed at the Church Road School in April 1938 in aid of church funds. Back row, left to right: Jack Doo, John Sanders, Howard Keeling, John Davies, Si Walker, Billy Pittaway, Tom Tromans and the Revd Frank Carr.

Front row: Eileen Phillips, Katherene Doo, Victoria Davies, Dorothy Birchall and Mary Sadler. Sitting at the front is young Betty Doo. Betty attended the first meeting of Dudley Little Theatre on 29 August 1947 and was a supporter of local amateur dramatics all her life. *(Betty Doo Collection)*

Geoff Smith assists in the promotion of Dudley's Real Ale Festival at Netherton Arts Centre, November 1987. Geoff worked at the Arts Centre until retiring in 1996.

Sarah Robinson, born in 1898, began her working life delivering bread and later became a postwoman. One of her first jobs was delivering ration books during the Second World War. At the end of the war she befriended a German PoW working on prefab construction in Hockley Lane, Baptist Gratz. The latter returned to Germany in 1948 and later became burgermeister of the town of Ballern. This led to several visits to and fro between Netherton and Ballern. This picture was posed outside Netherton post office in 1988 when Sarah celebrated her ninetieth birthday. *(May Oliver)*

Florence Cole was the daughter of William and Gertrude Cole and she lived with her parents at 1 St John's Street. Her father worked the family's farm at Lodge Farm and delivered milk to many parts of Netherton from there. She was photographed at St John's Chapel, next door to her home, in about 1990. She is beneath a plaque in memory of Mary Cole, placed there by her husband Alderman John Cole, thought to be Florence's great-uncle. In later life she lived alone at 1 St John's Street, behind the butcher's shop. She was last seen on 4 June 1999 and her disappearance has never been solved. She was a smart, intelligent woman, and although slightly reclusive, has been missed by many Nethertonians. *(NLHG)*

The Netherton Platoon of the 3rd Worcs. (Dudley) Battalion of the Home Guard enjoying their informal stand down party in December 1944. *(Megan Crofts)*

The shooting team of the Dudley Wood Home Guard photographed on the bowling green in front of Netherton Conservative Club during the war. Back row, left to right: Lawson Billingham, -?-, Ben Totney, -?-, Jack Tromans. Front row: David Taylor (second from left) and George Woodcock (fourth from left). Jack Tromans maintained a little black book of everyone's name and number and issue of rifles and ammunition. *(Owen Chilton)*

Remembrance Day at Primrose Chapel, 1989. Joe Guest greets Fred Homer and Tommy Tromans while the Revd Canon Wilcox talks to the Mayor of Dudley, Cllr Sam Davies. On this occasion a war memorial from Hingley's Ironworks was unveiled, following its removal to Primrose Chapel. *(Joe Guest)*

The Netherton Branch of the British Legion was represented by Messrs Robinson and Pearson at the celebrations for sixty years since the end of the Second World War in Stevens Park, Quarry Bank, 10 July 2005. The standard bearer was Mr Pearson Jnr. *(NW)*

The Netherton Carnival Queen's attendants during Coronation year, 1953. Left to right: Margaret Elwell, Jean Hipkiss, Rita Boulton, Jean Priest and June Robinson. Where's Jean Homer, the Carnival Queen? Answer: On the title page of *Netherton in Old Photographs*!. *(Harry Rose)*

Julie Sylvester was Carnival Queen on 13 June 1985 – the last carnival to be held in Netherton. She is flanked by her attendants: Sonia Kendrick and Sarah Hill. *(Margaret Sylvester)*

Pre-war carnival days took place to raise funds to support the local hospital. This picture was taken in about 1928 outside the Dolphin public house. The Pearly King in the front row is Frankie Gower, the son of the Dolphin licensees who are standing at the back. Just behind the clown is Agnes Parsons who supplied the picture via her sister. *(Sheila Hodgetts)*

A children's party organised at the Boat Inn, St Peter's Road, August 1933. The elderly lady in the centre of the picture is Granny Davenport and Nellie Dingley is on her lap. Next to Nellie are Dolly, Fred and Alice Shelton. The pub is illustrated on page 87 of *Netherton in Old Photographs. (Janet Stockton)*

On Whit Monday 1961 the regulars at the Junction Inn re-created a traditional trap outing to Kinver Edge. Harry Round, in the bowler hat, is the driver, and it was all in aid of charity. Note that the Labour Club, in its unrebuilt form, can be seen on the left, and Noah's Ark can be glimpsed in Cradley Road, on the right. *(Jimmy Round)*

Nethertonians at the Young Men's Institute – 'The 'Stute' – in Birch Terrace, *c*. 1948. Left to right: -?-, Wesley Slimm, Reg Willetts, Jim Warby, Ron Hall, Colin Rickards and Dennis Read. *(Lindsey Cooper)*

A wartime picture of the pub cricket teams from the King William (Cole Street) and the Lion. Walter Gregg, landlord of the King William, is seen standing second from right. The match was held at Hingley's Sports Ground, to raise money for men in the forces. *(Jack Brookes)*

The Brotherhood cricket team assembled in the Stoney Lane playing field, 1930. The team consisted of young men from Primrose Hill Chapel. Back row, left to right: Harry Cashmore, George Darby, Noah Hingley, Bill Darby, Ernie Allen. Front row: Tom Hughes, George Morgan, William Phillips, Matt Hingley, Barney Norton, Sidney Hill. *(Megan Crofts)*

The Second Netherton Scouts were formed at Primrose Hill just before the First World War and they are seen here outside the chapel. The establishment of the Guides followed soon afterwards. *(Megan Crofts)*

Netherton members of the local branch of the St John Ambulance Brigade in 1955/6 when Rose Wakeman was the branch president (see page 68). *(Rose Wakeman Collection)*

Parents and children at a 1953 Coronation party organised by the residents of Yew Tree Road and held at the Clydesdale Stamping Company's canteen. *(Megan Crofts)*

The Mayor of Dudley, Cllr Wakeman and his mayoress, Rose Wakeman, attend an ox-roast at the Yew Tree Hills public house, 1955. The pub, recently refurbished, was once a private house belonging to a colliery manager. *(Jean Wakeman Collection)*

The Netherton Liberal Club Male Voice Choir photographed in 1952 while singing at Trinity Methodist Chapel (Church Road). *(Malcolm Cartwright)*

Netherton Cricket Club members moving a hut from Saltwells School to the cricket ground in 1966. Left to right: Jack Doughty (a local teacher), Fred Rollason (author of the history of Netherton Cricket Club), his son Bryan Rollason, and Graham Armishure. President of NCC at the time was Fred Grainger, a well-known local butcher, who had a shop in Halesowen Road. *(W. Boyd)*

No survey of local people would be complete without another glimpse of Nethertonians at work. Here we see James Russell posing at his ironworks, the Withymoor Works of Swindell & Co., Northfield Road, 13 April 1907. James Russell was the son-in-law of George Dunn and is seen in the family photograph shown on page 8.

James Russell is seen again in this picture taken at Swindell & Co.'s works, 2 August 1907. He is standing on the right, next to the new gas engine which was being installed on this occasion. Unfortunately, although James is identified, there is no record of the names of the other men seen in the picture.
(Both Jean Wakeman Collection)

The millwrights and blacksmiths from Hingley's works in about 1910 – but definitely not at work! *(Ken Rock Collection)*

One of a series of photographs taken at Hingley's in about 1921 when equipment was being replaced. The furnaceman is removing slag that is coming over the fore-plate of a puddling furnace. Work in most of Netherton's workplaces was hot and dirty. *(NLHG)*

Left: James Morrison, a heat treatment specialist, hoists a steel product at Clydesdale Stampings in 1964. Morrison worked at the firm in the Marriott Road works for fourteen years. *(James Morrison)*

Clydesdale Stamping Co. was formed in 1929 in Clyde Street, Old Hill, hence the name. In 1936 the firm moved to the premises in Marriott Road, Netherton. The firm has expanded on the site and has been very successful in the specialised drop forging industry.

Below: Another view of the heat treatment shop at Clydesdale Stampings, 1961. Dennis Chilton is on the left, but the other two men have not been identified. *(Owen Chilton)*

Chapter Five
The Folks at Church & Chapel

Churches and chapels were the centres of Christian worship on Sundays, but most of them also provided a vast range of religious, educational and social activities all through the week – hence the variety of pictures featured in this chapter. Anglicans are to be found at St Andrew's, St Peter's and St John's; Methodists (Wesleyan, Primitive and New Connexion), Baptists (General and Particular) and Congregationalists were all to be found in at least one chapel and the Christadelphians also have a presence in Netherton.

The Revd Canon Frederick Wilcox sits at St Andrew's Church surrounded by his church choir, 1981.

After *Netherton in Old Photographs* was published, I received a few comments about the lack of pictures of the Fred Wilcox era at St Andrew's Church. This picture was taken in April 1994, with his wife, Joan, when Fred Wilcox retired. *(Joan Wilcox Collection)*

Canon Fred Wilcox appears again, this time surrounded by members of the Mothers' Union, 1986. Back row, left to right: J. French, P. Aston, P. Ashman, K. Edwards, M. Ashman, M. Walters. Middle row: D. Lissamore, R. Writtle, E. Hopper, B. Jones, S. Totney, M. Sanders, L. Glover, A. Hughes, A. Tilley. Front row: I. Shaw, F. Wellings, E. Ashman, H. Hale, Joan Wilcox, Fred Wilcox, M. Wheeler, B. Poole and S. Woodhouse.

The Young Mothers & Children Group photographed at Church House in 1994. Sue Cull, the organiser, is seen on the left clutching a baby and Joan Wilcox is seated in the middle of the scene. Church House has since been abandoned and the building has been put up for sale. A portion of the church has been screened from the main area of worship and now provides a meeting place. *(Both photographs on this page, and the previous page, Joan Wilcox Collection)*

Photographs of the folks at Messiah Baptist Chapel at Cinder Bank, seem few and far between so we have to be grateful for this glimpse of a harvest festival featuring the late Maisie Bloomer assisting in the sale of the harvest produce. *(Margaret and Bernard Sylvester)*

This big Sunday School anniversary picture features three Tromans sisters. It was taken at the back of Trinity Methodist Chapel in Church Road in the 1940s. The Wesleyan Methodist church did not actually adopt the name Trinity until 1991. *(Dot Tromans)*

Two pictures of the Sweet Turf Band. *Above:* Outside Netherton Lodge, the Old People's Home in St Andrew's Road; *below:* in Upton Street. The band was formed by Stanley Tibbetts, who can be seen in the middle of the top picture. On the left of the top picture is Mrs Burchell from the Cinder Bank post office who later married Mr Willetts. Both pictures were taken in the early 1970s. *(Brian Birchell)*

Above: This delightful period group is made up of the Swan Street Mission Choir standing in front of their tin tabernacle in the 1920s. Front row, left: Lucy Dingle. *Below:* The same shield seems to appear in this 1940s picture of a group at Swan Street inside the brick-built mission hall of 1932. Back row, left to right: -?-, Betty Hill, -?-, Joan Green, -?-, -?-, -?-, Robert Danks and Bruce Monkton. Front row: Mary Pritchard, Margaret Wall, Brenda Hancox, Dorothy Darby, Lucy White, Eileen Grosvenor, -?- and Doreen Hancox. Adults: Miss Hilda Parker and Mr Arthur Willetts.

The choir at the Swan Street Mission Hall in the 1990s. Back row, left to right: Fred Dingle (organist and son of Lucy Dingle, identified in the 1920s picture on previous page), Vic Darby, Michael Smith, Harry Parsonage, Muriel Flavell, Margaret and Arnold Province. Middle row: Daisy Hancox, Irene Darby, Doreen Jordan, -?-, -?-, Beryl Parsonage, Gladys Penn, Winnie Homer, Hilda Parker and Reg Penn. Front row: Charles Cartwright, Bessie Dingle, Elsie Holyoake, Lizzie Clarke, Olive Hamilton, Mary Lees, Gladys Spittle and Sarah Millard.

Left: The Mayor of Dudley, Cllr Sam Danks, stands between Mr and Mrs Colin Brown, a local steel stock-holder, at the Swan Street Mission Hall on the occasion of dedicating a new electronic console for the organ which had been donated by Mr Brown in 1953. (*Both Mission Hall Collection via Brian Payton*)

The Sunday School anniversary at Noah's Ark Methodist Chapel, Cradley Road, still seems to be going strong here in May 1990, but the chapel closed in March 2004. *(David Willetts)*

Two members of the Noah's Ark congregation receive long service awards at their chapel on 13 December 1986. Left to right: The Revd Brian Peters (minister at Noah's Ark), Frank Willetts (fifty years' service), the Revd Norman Owen (an ex-Nethertonian), Bill Detheridge (forty years' service), and Bob Crew (secretary of the Local Preachers Group). *(David Willetts)*

David Willetts with a model of Noah's Ark Chapel made by his father, Frank Willetts, who appears in the picture at the bottom of the previous page. David became particularly involved in youth work at Noah's Ark. *(NW)*

On 1 October 1977 the Noah's Ark Methodist Youth Club set out to collect pennies and then cover a table-tennis table with them, to raise money for church funds. Over 10,000 coins were collected and £105.83 was raised. The laying-out team included Rita Faulkner, Graham Faulkner, Linda Chilton, Tina Heath, Alison Capewell and Angela Cooper. The event was co-ordinated by David Willetts in his capacity as youth leader. *(David Willetts)*

Pictures from the Youth Club archives might provide us with the only surviving image of the interior of the Sunday School hall and its stage. Like the rest of the Noah's Ark complex, this is now being converted into apartments. The Sunday School building pre-dates the chapel and carries foundation stones dated 1898. On 14/15 May 1982 we see the hall being used for a tennis marathon – twenty-four hours of non-stop tennis was played by members of the youth club. The event raised £425. *(David Willetts)*

The Shell Group at Noah's Ark Chapel was a midweek youth club for Sunday School scholars, and here we find them putting on a Western evening on 21 September 1988. The leaders from the back row, left to right: Andrew Willetts, Jeremy Sharratt, Linda Chilton, and Jean Willetts. *(David Willetts)*

Here we see two contrasting pictures of the ladies from Primrose Hill Congregational Church. A group posing for a photograph in the church grounds, *c.* 1932. Back row, left to right: Mrs Simpson, Mrs Hill, Mrs Griffiths, Mrs Willetts, Mrs Timmington, Mrs Price, Mrs Stokes, Miss Brookes, Mrs Griffiths, Mrs Bennett. Front row: Mrs Griffiths, Mrs Shaw, Mrs Hughes, Mrs Bridgewater, Mrs Parry, Mrs Hill, Mrs Freeman, Mrs Shaw, Mrs Bussey, and possibly Miss Tilley. *(Megan Crofts)*

A 1950s group photographed on an outing. *(Joe Guest)*

A traditional anniversary, still featuring white dresses and the use of a platform, photographed at Cole Street Methodist Church in 1990. *(Geoff and Olive Smith)*

In contrast, here is a twenty-first century Sunday School anniversary in which the congregation turns round to face the stage and the Sunday School scholars present excerpts from *Joseph and his Amazing Technicolour Dreamcoat*, 20 June 2004. *(NW)*

There has been a long dramatic tradition at Cole Street Methodist Church, led by the Cole Street Concert and Drama Group. They have presented musical shows, pantomimes and nativity plays over the years. Here are three Cole Street angels from a Nativity play of the mid-1960s. Becky Smith was the angel in the middle. *(Geoff and Olive Smith)*

Every chapel and church are constantly raising funds. Here is the Men's Fireside Group from Cole Street Methodist Church at the bazaar held in November 1976. Left to right: Geoff Smith, Olive Smith, Jim Whitehouse, Rosemary Ward and Harry Felton. Shell-craft seems to have been a craze at the time! *(Geoff and Olive Smith)*

Chapter Six
The Folks at School

School pictures exist in most people's collections of old photographs. Sometimes, as in the 1931 example seen below, every scholar can be identified, but in others the faces appear anonymous but publication often results in some long-lost friend being identified by a reader on the far side of the world!

Netherton's school history is quite complicated, but after the passing of the 1870 Education Act, the newly formed Dudley School Board struggled to provide universal education in all parts of Netherton. In outlying districts like Darby End and Dudley Wood, schoolrooms had to be hired from existing Methodist Sunday Schools. In central Netherton the Church of England had already entered the educational field. Since then schools have gone through a never-ending process of change. Sometimes what was temporary – like the 'Iron Schools' – seemed to last forever, and other changes meant to be permanent – like middle schools quickly came and went.

The Council Boys' School, class 7, 1931. Back row, left to right: Messrs Horne, Plimmer, Aston, Howell, Darby, Willetts, Woodall, Willetts and Priest. Second row: Whitehouse, Edwards, Gill, Hingley, Robinson, Fred Homer (later a councillor), Russon and Robinson. Third row: Fred Shaw (teacher), Totney, Wheeler, Davies, Johnson, Barnes, Lavender, Knowles and Phillips. Front row: Ashman, Harrison, Ashman, Stroyde, Pritchards, Miles, Jack Phillips (who later kept the Blue Pig), Cox, Taylor, Clift and Jones. *(Mike Woodall)*

The 1908 school building on the corner of Church Road and the Halesowen road still dominates the centre of Netherton, although no longer used as a school. This was the last photograph taken at the school when the staff and pupils posed for the final time as Netherton Church of England Middle School, 1986. Three years later the building was sold for retailing use. *(Joan Wilcox Collection)*

Northfield Road Junior School looking down the side of the 1913 building towards the Savoy cinema in the 1980s. *(School Archives)*

The Northfield Road Junior School skittleball team, 1979/80. Back row, left to right: Ann Edwards, Joy Edge, Gail Kent, Tracey Alexandra, Sonia Jones. Front row: Julie Rothin, Clare Jeavons, Jayne Adams, Joanne Rock and Vicky Earl. *(Gail Kent)*

Unidentified members of the Northfield Road football team, 1981. They were trained by Tom Muncie. *(School Archives)*

During the 1980s Northfield Road Junior School presented some exciting pantomimes and shows. Here is a line up of the cast of *Aladdin*, July 1980. *(School Archives)*

Pupils from Northfield Junior School became involved in landscaping and tree-planting at the Halesowen road side of the former Goods station (see also page 42), December 1981. Cllr David Sparks and the architect and planner, A.A. Wood, join the children in watching some tree-planting. These trees are now substantial and hide the canal basin from the road. *(School Archives)*

Northfield Road Primary School, 1990s. *Above:* The annual Easter Bonnet parade, 1996. *Below:* A 'Greek Day' at Northfield Road in the 1990s provides a glimpse of additional temporary classroom accommodation in use at the time. *(Both School Archives)*

School dinners at Northfield Road Primary School in the early 1990s. In the photograph are Jacky Honey (left) and Mrs Sue Cartwright (right) who still runs the school kitchen. *(School Archives)*

Following the publication of *Netherton in Old Photographs*, the children in Year Six at Northfield Road Primary School became involved in a 'Netherton: Then and Now' project, in which the author was able to participate. The climax of the project was a show, performed on 11 and 12 July 2006.

Here we see Sophie Tromans, Jodie Edwards, Anthony Goodall, James Fottrell and Ashley Bowen from the cast of 'Netherton: Then and Now'. *(Express & Star)*

Christmas 1952 at Yew Tree Primary School was the first Christmas in the new school building. Left to right: Sylvia James as the Fairy Queen (with a dress and wand made by her parents), Elves: Mark ?, Geoffrey Jones, -?-, Alan Broome and Santa played by David Jones. (*Sylvia Lucas*)

Staff and head teacher, Miss Joan White, at Yew Tree Primary School in the early 1980s.

Bowling Green Junior School opened in 1953, and these photographs were taken three years later. Here we see the sports team of 1956. Back row, left to right: Mr Horridge (headmaster), Mr Cotterill, Miss Sutcliffe and Mr Lilley. Middle row: Peter Moore, John Hall, Patricia Pugh, Dorothy Childs, Paul Timmington and George Benbow. Front row: Paul Pugh, Ronald Humphries, David Spencer, Ann Smith, Shirley Wood and Pauline Lloyd. *(Pat Hughes)*

Kitchen staff at Bowling Green in the 1950s: -?-, Mrs Williams (cook), Gwen Lucas, -?-, Doris ?, Mrs Hiscox (lunchtime supervisor) and Daisy (Maude) Pugh. *(Pat Hughes)*

The school choir at Bowling Green Primary School in the mid-1950s, photographed on a set of removable steps on the school stage. The choir was trained by Mr Harvey who seems to have evaded the photographer.

The netball team at Bowling Green Primary school, *c.* 1975. Back row, left to right: Jane ?, Julie Homer, Andrea Pritchard, and Dawn Tipton. Front row: Dawn Taylor, Debbie Weaver and Vivian Wakeman. *(Both Vivian Wakeman Collection)*

Saltwells Infants School started life in January 1964 in the old woodwork and cookery huts of the 'Iron Schools', but by Easter the new school was ready and this picture was taken on 26 May 1964 at the official opening. The Mayor of Dudley, Cllr W.J.K. Griffiths, joins an art class after his colleague Alderman Hillman had performed the opening ceremony as Chairman of the Education Committee. *(Clarice Walters Collection)*

The school choir at Saltwells Infants School stole the show at the Dudley Festival of Music and Drama in March 1966, winning the competition in the infants category. Here the choir poses with headteacher, Clarice Walters, on the right. *(Clarice Walters Collection)*

Headteacher Clarice Walters and the
Alliband triplets (Stephen, Philip and
Paul) and the Hill twins (John and Peter)
at Saltwells Infant School, January 1969.
(*Clarice Walters Collection*)

Under the reorganisation of schools in
Dudley, Saltwells Infants became Saltwells
First School taking pupils aged from five
to eight and passed them on to Bowling
Green Middle School which provided
for the nine to thirteen age group. This
changed again in 1984 when Saltwells
First School was closed and by merging
it with Bowling Green, a new school was
created on the Bowling Green site. The
new school opened in September 1984
and was called Netherbrook Primary
School taking pupils aged from five to
twelve. Later a nursery was added. The
name Netherbrook was cleverly invented
by Clarice Walters.

Country dancing in the playground at Netherbrook Primary School in July 1992. In the
background are the school buildings originally provided in 1954 when the school was
opened as Bowling Green Primary School. Bowling Green was originally a small hamlet built
alongside Bowling Green Road, close to the Mousesweet Brook and Netherton's southern
boundary. (*Clarice Walters Collection*)

Class 1ii at Netherbrook Primary School in 1992, including Daniel Church, Jodie Ashman, Luke Doley, Robert Westwood, Michelle Bart, Sophie Emery, Rebecca Johnson, Kelly Dunn, Stacey Wilkinson, Shane Price, Kristina Edwards, Ashley Bowen, Melissa Andrews, Dipisha Patel, Joanne Langston, Adam Duncan, Daniel Doman, Duncan Binnion, Dale Appleby, Amy Nash and Matthew Carter. Note the extensive playing fields stretching across towards Norwich Road. *(Netherbrook School Archives)*

The dinner ladies at Netherbrook Primary School, 1992. Here we see Margaret Cole, Gill Hunt, Kath Wright, Maureen Virgo, K. Biggins, G.A. Fox, S.M. Harold and D. Parton. The pool was a much-used location for school photographs. *(Clarice Walters Collection)*

The kitchen staff at Netherbrook Primary School, 1992. In this photograph we see Mrs I. Cunningham, Mrs G.C. Wright, Mrs E.M. Scarratt and Mrs J.E. Coleman. *(Clarice Walters Collection)*

This very thorough survey of the staff at Netherbrook Primary School in 1992 is completed with a portrait of the cleaning staff: Mrs K. Coates, Mrs E. Allen, Mrs L. Sherwood, Mrs A. White, Mrs J. Wood and Mrs D. Nixon. *(Clarice Walters Collection)*

The primary school in Dudley Wood Road has a history stretching back to 1931 when it was opened as a pioneering open air school for 200 children. Going back further, the school replaced a Church of England Primary School which had operated in the primitive wooden buildings of St Barnabas' Mission. This aerial view, dating from about 1970, shows these school grounds in relation to the vast area of derelict land behind it that had been the site of Saltwells Colliery Pit no. 19. *(School Archives)*

One of the many maypole dancing pictures from Dudley Wood Junior School. This 1946 picture shows the original style of the classrooms with their access to fresh air, and the open land behind the school. The verandas of the classrooms were later turned into corridors. *(School Archives)*

Anne Cross, lady in waiting, crowns the Dudley Wood Primary School May Queen, Janet Sidaway, in May 1947. As usual the crowning ceremony was followed by the performance of folk dances, in which the pupils had been coached by Miss A. Manning. *(School Archives)*

Sometimes the May festivals at Dudley Wood Primary School featured pageants and plays. Here, in 1953, the Coronation year, we can see the performance included St George slaying the dragon. Note that the verandas are now filled in. *(School Archives)*

Pupils of Dudley Wood First School, as it was known in June 1981, assemble in the playground to welcome Cradley Heath speedway riders Erik Gunderson and Bruce Penhall to the school fête. In the background is Dudley Wood Road that many fans traversed to reach the speedway stadium. *(School Archives)*

Dudley Wood First School in June 1981. This time we see the crowd assembled in the hall to watch Cradley Heath speedway rider Erik Gunderson, receive a presentation from pupils, watched by headteacher Pauline Woodhall. *(School Archives)*

Dudley Wood Primary School. *Above:* Mrs Cree and her pupils pose for a school photograph, 1977. *Below:* Staff pose for a picture a decade later. Back row, left to right: Gina Hammond, John Taylor, Alison Royal, Jenny Atherton, Mary Roberts, Annabelle Thompson, Anthea Collinge, and Jill Haycox. Front row: Helen Markham, Pam Fenney, Pauline Woodhall (headteacher), Freda Lowe, and Ruth Scott. *(School Archives)*

Saltwells Secondary Modern School was opened in 1962 in a brand new building in Bowling Green Road. It is now an education centre.

Here we see the under-16 football team in the 1980s. Back row, left to right: Mr P. Cooper, S. Payne, R. Dunning, T. Hughes, E. Jeavons, S. Carolan, J. Slater, D. Dingley. Front row: K. Billingham, S. Price, S. Male, C. Brookes, H. Johnson. Saltwells Secondary School later amalgamated with Hillcrest. *(John Brookes)*

Hillcrest Secondary School girls' hockey team, 1978/9. *(Vivian Wakeman)*

Hillcrest Secondary School was opened in Simms Lane in 1958, and was rebranded as a community college at the end of the 1970s.

Mo Brennan came to the school as headteacher in 2000 and left in 2007 to go to the Barr Beacon Language College. These photographs were taken in 2005 when she was made Dame Mo Brennan in recognition of her services to education. She is seen to the right with Hillcrest scholars, and below with Hillcrest prefects Carl Hale and Kylie Jones.
(Express & Star)

The nursery, built in Netherton's park, began life as a pioneering attempt to provide childcare for working mothers during the Second World War. It was provided with a typical Ministry of Supply building, but enjoyed a very attractive setting in the park close to the Arch Hill Street entrance. *(Nursery Archives)*

The old nursery had a community room added in the mid-1980s and then, in 1995, new buildings were provided and it was reopened as a family centre. The 1940s buildings were demolished. Left: Dora Bryan, seen here with Chris Catanach, came along on 16 November 1995 to officially open Netherton's new family centre.

Balloons decorated the entrance to the family centre when it opened. In 2004 the facilities in the park were redesignated as a Children's Centre. Its greatly expanded work now includes parenting classes for adults.
(Centre Archives)

A successful nursery enlists the help of the parents. Here we see kitchen supervisor Olive Shelton (left) using some help from colleague Joyce Anslow and a couple of parents on the occasion of the opening of a new community room.

Parents, councillors and children join in opposing the closure of the nursery in 1982. Mr and Mrs Cooksey are in the back row while their son Steven is in the front (right). Sandra Hadfield, second from left, is behind her son Stephen. The mayor, Cllr David Ranceford-Hadley sits some children on his knee, and other councillors present include Messrs Rahman, Davies and Andrews. *(Nursery Archives)*

Park Nursery, Netherton, 1967. The note on the back of this picture tells us that the following ladies appear: Margaret Lee, Mrs Mackintosh, Nurse Coulter, Mrs Taylor, Mrs Round, Miss Timmings, Mrs Cornes, Mrs Martin, Heather Wood, Beverley ?, Yvonne Guest and Jacqueline Callaghan. *(Nursery Archives)*

In this 1995 picture the nursery has become a family centre. On the right is Chris Catanach, head of the centre, and on the left is Hilary Briggs. *(Nursery Archives)*

Chapter Seven

Around the Clubs

In this chapter we take a quick look at the political clubs of Netherton: Labour, Liberal and Conservative, and revisit the local Toc H branch. The political clubs have been much more than just a focus for the support of particular party – they have been sporting and social clubs with a wide variety of activities – some of which are represented by the pictures on the following pages.

The 1962 frontage of Netherton Labour Club on the Halesowen road between the Junction Inn and Malcolm's hairdressing shop. This replaced the Edwardian shopfronts glimpsed in the picture on page 83. *(NW)*

Netherton Labour Club. A Netherton branch of the Labour Party was formed about 1916, and members used to meet in the Lamp Tavern on Bath Hill, Dudley. At the end of the First World War they rented the shops at 365, 366 and 367 Halesowen Road – the building between the Junction Inn of 1905 and the parade of shops of 1908.

A group of about sixteen people then formed the Netherton Labour Club and Workers Institute, and in 1920, they purchased these premises. The first trustees included William Hughes, Thomas Newton and Mark Fletcher, the latter probably being able to assist in the matter of the club obtaining a license.

The club retained its original appearance until 1962 when it was entirely remodelled – creating its present façade – at a cost of £16,000. In 1983 a lounge extension was added at a cost of £40,000, and the clubroom was further renovated in 1988. Roy Lea was club secretary during these refurbishments.

This picture was probably taken on 24 September 1910 behind 30 St Thomas's Street, just over a week before the official opening of the Liberal Club. A list of those included in the picture survives but not in any order! Cllrs Little and Greaves are among the members of the committee present. The tree in the background was removed before the opening.

The same location was used on Monday 3 October 1910 when the Liberal Club was officially opened. In the centre are Mr Arthur Hooper MP, his wife and his daughter, Winifred. J.W. Wilson MP and the local councillors are also present. The picture was taken by Walter Wootton of Quarry Bank. (*Both Club Archive via John Mason*)

Netherton Liberal Club

The Liberals in Netherton were enjoying some success in the years before the First World War, and early in 1910 they seem to have decided to open a Liberal Club, partly to celebrate Messrs Little and Greaves's success in being elected to the council. At a meeting in March, various possible locations and existing buildings were identified and committee members resolved to inspect them.

At one stage it was decided to build a corrugated-iron building on land belonging to Mr Deeley at Eagle Hill. The committee then became more ambitious and contemplated a brick building, meanwhile considering two houses as temporary premises. One of these was the house at 30 St Thomas's Street belonging to Mr Dando. In fact this became the Liberal Club's permanent home, calling itself the Netherton Liberal Cub & Institute. From the beginning, one of the necessities was a billiard table, even if this meant planning immediate alterations to the premises. News of all this progress was made public at a meeting in the Public Hall on 4 July 1910.

There were many matters to resolve. A steward, Mr Whitehouse, had to be appointed at a wage of 5s a week, a constitution had to be created, and the ladies, who were not going to be able to use the club, had to be persuaded to help furnish the place and make tea at the grand opening.

The opening took place on Monday 3 October 1910, with the MPs A.G. Hooper and J.W. Wilson as guests of honour. From its inception the club seems to have operated successfully and facilities and extensions were all improved, including, in 1912, the opening of a bowling green. The substantial club room at the rear of the building was opened by a member of the Mander family from Wolverhampton on 26 July 1913.

The football club was started in about 1919 by Horace Greaves who was a teacher at Northfield Road, later becoming headmaster at the 'Iron Schools'. They first played at Blackbrook, and later at a ground near Cinder Bank.

The Liberal Club building at 30 St Thomas's Street, decorated for the Coronation in June 1953. The club is still in this location but the building has been modified over the years. (Harry Rose)

The Netherton Liberal Club football team in the 1930s, photographed at the rear of the club in St Thomas's Street. Mr Hingley (left of the middle two players) was the club steward for many years.

Trophy night for the Netherton Liberal Club billiards team, probably photographed in 1934. The main trophy stills exists on the club premises today. *(Both Club Archives via John Mason)*

Netherton Conservative Club

The club began life as the Netherton Conservative Working Men's Club and its first premises were opened at the Willows in Cradley Road on 29 November 1886 by Mr Brooke Robinson, Dudley's MP.

The club moved to its present premises in 1913 by purchasing Netherton House, which had formerly been the home of George Dunn. At this time a company was registered to run the club and the original five directors were named as Owen Francis Grazebrook, Thomas Hartshorne, Joseph Smith, John Walter Barnsley and Thomas Jones. The pride of the club was its ballroom with sprung floor, up on the first storey. This floor was severely tested when the Home Guard used the room for drill practice during the Second World War!

From its heyday in the 1930s, the club declined in the post-war era and in 1953 the chairman, F.A. Faulkner, warned its thirty members that the decline might be fatal. Several members took up the challenge and began a drastic refurbishment of the premises. The renewed club was reopened on 5 November 1954 by Sir Hugh Chance. By the 1960s, membership had climbed to over 200 once again. At this event – and the opening of 1913 – were the Newns brothers, Rupert and Sidney, both of whom were members for over fifty years.

The Bowling Green outside the club also had its ups and downs. At one time Cllr Noel Evans had to keep sheep on it to graze the neglected green, but it was revitalised during the 1960s.

Netherton Conservative Club occupies a house that had once belonged to George Dunn (see page 65), although rebuilt in 1913 for club use. The drive in front of the building follows its original course but now encircles the bowling green. *(NW)*

Don Williams (second from the left), the prospective Conservative candidate for Dudley East, re-opens the bar at the Halton Road premises of the Conservative Club after a further period of refurbishment led by Jim Newton, John Davies and Walter Sidaway.

On the right, behind the bar at the Netherton Conservative Club, we find Ronald and Ruth Woodall, the club stewards, assisted by Minnie Davies on the left, 1960s.

The annual harvest festival was an important event at the Netherton Conservative Club. Here we see Ronald Woodall, the club steward, accept the winning marrow from Freddie Portman in about 1960. Freddie Portman ran a sweet shop next to Grainger's the butchers, opposite the junction of Simms Lane with Cinder Bank.

Fred and Minnie Davies grasp a box full of fruit and Fred Homer displays a loaf at the Netherton Conservative Club harvest festival, c. 1960. Ruth Woodall and Jimmy Glazebrook look on.

Members of the dominoes team from the Netherton Conservative Club are seen here with the Netherton Domino League Trophy, handed out at the Labour Club, in about 1980. Left to right: Jim Newton (league chairman), Jim Glazebrook (league president), Malcolm Taylor (captain of the winning team form the Packhorse public house), and Bernard Hotchkiss (league organiser).

The Crib League Trophy, seen in the top picture, can still be seen today at the Netherton Conservative Club. Left to right: Mike Woodall, Ray Darby and Jimmy Newton. *(NW)*

Above: The West Midlands Conservative Bowling League Trophy was won in 1928 by the Netherton Conservative Club bowlers. They seen here outside the club.

Below: The club and its green survive today but as can be see in this recent photograph, bowlers no longer seem to look the same!

On page 157 of *Netherton in Old Photographs* you will find a picture of the original Netherton Toc H headquarters near the cricket ground. Having 'received its lamp' in 1937 the group had to move in 1943 and came to this little hut at 53 Griffin Street. It was purchased by Fred H. Jennings and given to Toc H for use during his lifetime.

A Netherton Toc H boys' camp at Astley Burf in 1949. The older generation who had first gone there as lads, then took the next generation. Back row, left to right: Ernie Harvey, Sam Bennett, Frank Walters, Harold Farmer, Fred Davenport, ? Price, Eric Jeavons, Wesley Garratt, Selwyn Johnson, Jeff Edwards, Wesley Jennings (son of Fred H. Jennings who had provided the Toc H building), Laurie Jennings (brother of Fred H. Jennings) and Leslie Davenport. First left on the second row is Arthur Foxall who began by helping out when he was fourteen. Two years later he joined Toc H and remained in the organisation all his life. (*Wesley Garratt*)

Chapter Eight
Darby End

Darby End, like Dudley Wood, seems rather remote from the centre of Netherton, and therefore has its own identity. Northfield Road, which begins in the heart of Netherton, reaches a crossroads from whence it continues as Withymoor Road. At the same crossroads, Cole Street continues as St Peter's Road, once known as Bumblehole Road. This crossroads is the centre of Darby End, and the village runs from there down into the valley of the Mousesweet Brook – a valley once shared by the Dudley–Old Hill railway line, but now the boundary between Dudley and Sandwell. Legend has it that nailers came to area from Derbyshire (i.e. they were 'Derby Hands'). Belper Row seems to have been named to make them feel at home! Whatever its origins, the settlement was well inhabited by the second half of the nineteenth century and housing extended along Belper Row, Double Row and Hadleys Fold, as well as the main roads of Withymoor Road and Cole Street. Gill Street was a later addition.

A Darby End Methodist Society existed as early as 1810 and the first Cole Street Wesleyan Methodist chapel was built in 1821. It was the folks from Cole Street who promoted the Wesleyan cause in the centre of Netherton several decades later. A New Connexion Methodist chapel was built in Northfield Road in 1837, next to Swindell's Withymoor Iron Works. This was Providence which was later moved to the Black Country Museum. The Church of England seems to have become aware of the growth of Darby End and responded by building a Sunday School/National School in 1871. From this grew the St Peter's Church we know today.

Events followed a similar pattern to those in Dudley Wood. When the 1870 Education Act created the Dudley School Board, the board seems to have instantly rented space in the Methodist Sunday School. Thus the first secular-based education to come to Darby End began in Cole Street in the 1870s – long before the better known facilities were developed in the 'Iron Schools'. Once again we are reminded of how much Darby End must have grown by that time.

Darby Enders must have walked to pits and iron works in neighbouring areas, rather then have found work on their doorstep, perhaps helping to maintain the rather village-like geography of the place. Twentieth-century housing has rather changed that. There are no longer watercress beds in the valley of Mousesweet Brook, or marl holes to sustain local brickworks. Canal arms and railway embankments have been swept away. What remains is the detachment – Darby End still seems slightly separated from everywhere else!

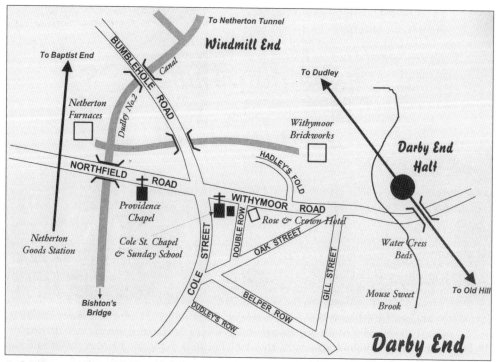

A sketch map of Darby End. An 1865 map shows Darby End as a well-established community in the triangle between Cole Street, Oak Street and Withymoor Road, plus Belper Row and the Hadley's Fold area. Gill Street was added towards the turn of the century and Stanhope Street/Stafford Street came later. The Mousesweet Brook formed the eastern boundary of Darby End, Netherton, and of Worcestershire, so Darby End Halt, when provided in 1905, was technically in Rowley Regis in Staffordshire. *(Map by Roger Crombleholme)*

Neighbours and friends of Joseph and Maria Timmington help celebrate their golden wedding at the Golden Cross pub in the 1950s. Joseph worked at Hingley's, but during the war Maria had worked in Darby End loading and unloading canal boats. *(Sheila Hodgetts)*

The Wesleyan Methodists built the first Darby End Chapel in 1821, but like many buildings in the area, it was affected by subsidence. Its replacement, seen here, was opened on 29 February 1904. The final service in this building took place on 14 May 1950 and the congregation moved into the Sunday School building until the present chapel opened on 3 October 1959. *(Bert Beard Collection)*

The Cole Street Sunday School building in Withymoor Road, after the congregation had moved into their new chapel, on the right of this picture, 1960s. The Darby End Board School used the premises on weekdays between the early 1870s and 1885. Beyond is the Rose & Crown Hotel, one of the loftiest buildings in Darby End. *(Dudley Archives)*

The Rose & Crown Hotel in Withymoor Road, 1960s. This grand building was built in 1901, replacing an older public house on the same site. It has now been converted to flats, but still dominates the area. The 1841 census tells us that Job Bird was the publican then operating on this site, and he was followed by his widow, Ann. She continued to run the pub until her death in 1868 at the age of eighty-five. Job and Ann had an unmarried daughter named Esther who ran the pub until 1874 when it was transferred to her sister-in-law, Louisa Bird. The Rose & Crown changed hands in about 1900 and was bought by John Dunn who also bought all the frontage along to Oak Street and some cottages in Double Row. A daughter of John Dunn named Annie, and her husband, Mr McDonald, opened a fish shop next door. John Dunn is presumed to have built the red brick building seen here, which was eventually owned by Ansells. (Information supplied by Mavourneen Heritage and Carl Higgs.) (W. Boyd)

A Sunday School anniversary parade from Providence Chapel, Darby End, 1966. The group are seen marching past Lewis's in Northfield Road. Lewis's employed quite a few female blacksmiths. On the right is David White, Sunday School superintendent. (Jack Phipps)

This picture of a Cole Street Chapel Sunday School anniversary parade of the early 1960s helps us understand how some places change more than others. In this instance the junction of Oak Street, along which they are walking, and Belper Row, seems to have changed, but all the buildings in the background do in fact still stand. *(Geoff and Olive Smith)*

Providence Chapel, once in Northfield Road, now resides in its new home at the Black Country Living Musuem. Not all the bricks survived the relocation and had to be supplemented by identical bricks made available by the demolition of the Wesley Chapel in Wolverhampton Street, Dudley. Providence had been built by the Methodists of the New Connexion in 1837 and survived in Darby End until 1974. The spiritual needs of Darby End were therefore served by St Peter's, and by three groups of Methodists: Providence (of the New Connexion), Cole Street (of the Wesleyans), and by the independent Wesley Bible Institute (see page 145 of *Netherton in Old Photographs*). *(NW)*

The corner of Gill Street seen from Withymoor Road in the early 1960s. Gill Street was developed in the 1890s on the track of a former ropeway or tramway that linked pits with the Withymoor Brick Works. Withymoor Road seems to narrow as it descends into the shallow valley of Mousesweet Brook. The building at the end of Gill Street still has the distinctive angled corner but is no longer Mrs Cole's shop. *(Dudley Archives)*

Gill Street today still includes some interesting housing built at the end of the nineteenth century and into the early twentieth century. It is seen here from the Belper Row end of the street. For some reason the children in Gill Street went to Church Road School rather than the 'Iron Schools', enhancing Gill Street's reputation as being a 'refined' part of Darby End. *(NW)*

Darby End Halt was opened on the Dudley–Old Hill railway in 1905 and was perched on top of the embankment above Withymoor Road. This 1962 picture shows a Dudley-bound train at the halt a year before the passenger service ceased. Over forty years later this embankment has disappeared and all trace of the bridge has vanished. On the extreme right is the wall of a bridge over the Mousesweet Brook. *(Peter Shoesmith/Author's Collection)*

The same location today. The barrier on the left-hand side of Withymoor Road reminds us that the road is crossing the Mousesweet Brook at this point and the road (now widened and straightened) becomes Gawne Road as it passes into Rowley Regis. The site of the watercress beds is still to be found on the right, but vegetation now obscures the view of Doulton's pipeworks, and the surrounding industrial area. *(NW)*

Although this picture is damaged, it provides us with a rare glimpse of the watercress beds at Darby End. In the background it is possible to make out the abutment of the railway bridge. In the foreground is Henry Dean, and behind him is the family of Solomon Danks. The latter obtained an agreement with the GWR in 1884, by whom he was employed as an engine driver, to live in the cottage and cultivate the watercress beds. At the time the road was called Dog Lane and as the cottage was on the far bank of the brook, it was technically in Rowley Regis. *(Alan Pritchard)*

Bert Phipps in the backyard at 12 and 13 Double Row, Darby End. Billy Whale (aged three) and Jack Phipps (aged five) are in the foreground. The fish boxes drying on the roof belonged to Jim Darby who ran a little wooden fish and chip shop in Double Row, just opposite nos 12 and 13. *(Jack Phipps)*

Bert Phipps and Billy Darby are
out in Oak Street, Darby End,
with their barrow collecting wood
for a fire to celebrate VE Day.

VE Day street party in Oak Street, Darby End, 8 May 1945. Included in the crowd are:
Maureen Taylor of Oak Street, Mrs Brant of Oak Street, Ginnie Harris of Double Row,
Charlotte Phipps of Double Row, Kelly Chater of Oak Street and Ann Phipps (aged one) of
Double Row. *(Both Jack Phipps Collection)*

The King William Inn, 9 Cole Street, Darby End. William Bayliss was landlord here in 1900, but this photograph was taken in the 1930s. *(Sheila Hodgetts)*

The original King William was replaced with this more modern version, which has now closed. This photograph taken in 2006. Note the proximity of Cole Street Methodist Church on the left. *(NW)*

Chapter Nine
Dudley Wood & Mushroom Green

The southernmost part of Netherton consists of several small communities, each once enjoying their own identity. The oldest settlement is Mushroom Green, scattered across the ground which rises from the Cradley Pool (the one-time flooded valley of the Black Brook) up to Quarry Road. At some stage, probably in the 1860s, someone tried to replace Mushroom Green by laying out the 'New Village' – now preserved as street name in the 1930s estate that replaced the original New Village. Slightly to the east of New Village is Dudley Wood Road.

By the end of the nineteenth century a small hamlet had grown up at the junction of Dudley Wood Road with Quarry Road but as the 1900s progressed new houses were built along Dudley Wood Road creating a rather linear settlement. Dudley Wood was really put on the map by the opening of Cradley Heath Stadium – entirely incorrectly named as it was definitely built on the Netherton side of the Mousesweet Brook!

The Earl of Dudley's railway system penetrated this area with lines that served the numerous pits of Saltwells Colliery, and its main line that passed through Mushroom Green parallel with Quarry Road until turning south to head for the GWR at Cradley Heath. A branch crossed Quarry Road between the Victoria Inn and the St Barnabas' Mission and headed for the Providence Iron Works at Newtown, Old Hill.

In 2005 one chainshop survives in Mushroom Green. It is preserved as an outpost of the Black Country Living Museum. Here we see Ron Moss providing a conducted tour in 2005. *(NW)*

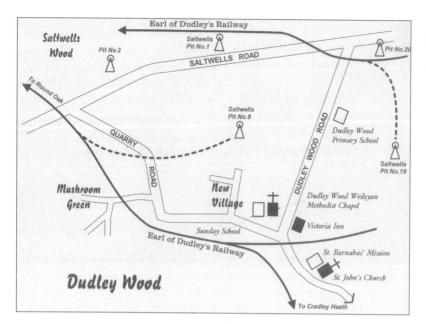

A sketch map
of Dudley
Wood.
*(Map by Roger
Crombleholme)*

The gateway to Mushroom Green. George Jasper (on the right) stands in front of the family's shop in the late 1930s. The shop occupied the front room of 97 Mushroom Green and was built in the 1930s. Emma Jasper can be seen in the doorway and was well known for her home-made ice cream. The Earl of Dudley's railway is seen on the right and trains were usually propelled towards Cradley Heath with the engine at the rear, so a flagman protected these open crossings. The line closed in 1952. The cottage on the left, Sadie Dunn's cottage, is still there, but the Jaspers' shop is now a private house. Note the garden fence reinforced with enamel signs! *(Julie Tonkin Collection)*

This picture was taken in the garden behind Jaspers' shop at 97 Mushroom Green and shows an early 1930s May Queen event. Lily Ness was May Queen attended by Hilda Cutler and Jean Westwood. The others are Lily Chater, Jack Wycherley, May Wilkes, Minnie Nicklin, Gwen Dunn, Kathy Weaver, Hilda Thompson, Kenneth Haines, -?- and Laura Billingham. It shows the extent to which Mushroom Green was an independent community with its own institutions.

A tug-of-war organised among Mushroom Greeners on Smith's Field in the late 1940s or early '50s. John and Winnie Jasper, the children of George and Emma (seen opposite), are in the centre of the picture. The building on the right is 76 Mushroom Green and has been in the Hancox family for four generations. The buildings on the left are on the far side of the earl's railway and can be found today by exploring Oxley Close. *(Both Julie Tonkin Collection)*

The chainshop in Mushroom Green that is preserved today once belonged to the Kendrick family. This view looking across the gardens towards that chainshop must have been taken about the turn of the twentieth century before the Kendricks had extended their house. *(Ron Moss Collection)*

The Kendrick Family of 14 Mushroom Green outside their home about 1910. Mr Kendrick Snr who started the family business is seated on the left, and his son William who was alive until fairly recent times is standing next to him. *(Ron Moss Collection)*

The Earl of Dudley's railway is crossing the centre of this picture in a shallow cutting. Beyond it, on the far side of Quarry Road, we can see the houses in Dudley Wood Road. On the right is the Victoria Inn. This, and some subsequent pictures, were taken about 1905 before steps appear to have been taken to improve Dudley Wood.

Florence Bradley is seen here making small chain in the chainshop next to 70 Mushroom Green. She was an outworker for the Hancox family. *(Ron Moss Collection)*

This view looks up Dudley Wood Road and reveals just how much this area was affected by subsidence (compare this with picture on page 21 of *Netherton in Old Photographs*). The railway crossed the road at the junction in front of the Victoria Inn and passed behind the ·wooden building of St Barnabas' Mission.

Here we see the railway passing a building that stood just behind the Victoria Inn, and the track heads straight towards the Providence Works (Penn's) at Old Hill. The desolate wastes to the left of the track became St Luke's football pitch, the fairground, and eventually the speedway stadium. Now residential development has taken place and Stadium Drive and Racemeadow Crescent have been created.

Some of the tilted houses in Dudley Wood Road survived until the 1970s and this one was very noticeable as it stood opposite the entrance to the speedway stadium and adjacent to Dudley Wood Methodist Church. New houses now occupy this site. *(Ivan Homer)*

The Victoria, Dudley Wood, as it is today. The Bridgewater family has owned the Victoria since the late nineteenth century, and the Victoria Brewery that was once associated with it. George Bridgewater who was running the pub and brewery in the 1930s later joined forces with Joseph Sidaway in setting up the company that developed the speedway. *(NW)*

Left: No. 39 Dudley Wood Road was a shop set amid a row of terraced houses that seem to have been built in the 1907–10 period. This picture was taken in 1928 and shows Mrs Lily Dunn, who ran the shop, with her two sons, George and James. James Dunn became a well-known butcher in Netherton.
(Joan Homer)

Below: The Edwardian houses of Dudley Wood Road, 2006. Lily Dunn's shop can be identified by the white straight lintel above the modernised window; the front wall has not changed! These twentieth-century additions to Dudley Wood extended the hamlet up towards Saltwells Road. Behind these houses was an area made derelict by Saltwells Colliery no. 19 and no. 15 pits, but it is now covered with houses. *(NW)*

Dudley Wood Road looking towards Saltwells Road, revealing the houses on the left-hand side of the road, opposite Lily Dunn's shop. The photograph was taken on 26 May 1963 and the parade was part of the Mayor's Civic Sunday celebrations. The service was held in St John's Church, Dudley Wood. *(Jeff Parkes)*

The Dudley Wood Methodist Operetta Company bringing entertainment to Dudley Wood in the 1930s. A number of well-known locals are on stage, including Luke Walters, Harry Johnson, Lawson Billingham and Harry Griffiths. *(Clarice Walters)*

Dudley Wood Football Club, the 'Vics', *c.* 1912 – champions of the Cradley Heath & District League. On the front row, on the captain's left, is Luke Walters, who went on to play for West Bromwich Albion. *(Clarice Walters)*

Cradley Heath Speedway Stadium in Dudley Wood Road. The high ground in the background was an old pit-bank, known locally as 'Scotsman's Hill'. This picture was taken in the mid-1960s after a period when the track had closed. The track originally opened on 21 June 1947 and closed finally in 1995. Barratt Homes began a long battle to build houses on the site against opposition from just about everybody. House construction began in 2002. *(W. Boyd)*

The Dudley School Board was established in 1871 and by 1873 it had arranged for a Dudley Wood School to be provided in the Methodist Church's wooden Sunday School building. Pupils are photographed outside the building in 1928, three years before the present Dudley Wood School was opened. *(School Archives)*

A Wesleyan Methodist Society may have been established in Mushroom Green as early as 1810 and documentation survives relating to the 'Sermons' (Sunday School anniversary) of May 1829. Later in that year it seems that the congregation moved to Dudley Wood Road. The building into which they moved appears in the background of one or two photographs but we really know very little about it. In 1866 work was started on a wooden Sunday School building – about which we know a lot more as it survived until 1959. From the 1870s until 1931 it also accommodated the local Board School.

The wooden school building belonging to the Wesleyan Methodists in all its ramshackle glory! It was built on brick piers but the pitch pine walls were a constant problem. Between the extensions were the boys' and girls' entrances. It seems amazing that it almost lasted a century. *(Alan Smith)*

Dudley Wood Methodist Chapel was bravely built at the end of Dudley Wood Road much affected by subsidence at the turn of the nineteenth century. This building replaced an earlier one that may well have been damaged by subsidence. Foundation stones were laid on 17 June 1907 and it was opened on 23 October 1907. (See page 147 of *Netherton in Old Photographs*). Here we see the chapel on 5 April 2004, about a year before the last service was held in the building. *(NW)*

The Sunday School anniversary at the Dudley Wood Methodist Chapel, May 1950. The chap second from the right on the front row is Jim Bradley who is currently chief steward at the church. (See also page 157). *(Alan Smith)*

The old wooden school building was demolished in 1959 and a new hall was built in its place. Here we see the Revd Arthur Hoof and Stanley Griffiths, the architect, watching Ralph Smith open the door of the new Sunday School on 24 June 1961. *(Alan Smith)*

After the last service in the 1907 chapel, held on 8 May 2005, the building was demolished and the congregation made plans to continue in the Sunday School building of 1961 vintage. A new entrance was built from Quarry Road and on 16 December 2006 the 'new' chapel was opened. Here we see Martin Shenton, the architect involved, handing over the keys to Jim Bradley and Walter Westbury who was the oldest member of the congregation. *(Express & Star)*

When Dudley Wood Primary School opened on 15 April 1931 it was regarded as a pioneering open-air school with classrooms which had french doors providing light and access to fresh air. In this early 1950s picture the boys are enjoying the fresh air while exercising on the ladder stand. *(School Archives)*

The school took on the task of maintaining the local tradition of having a May Queen (see page 147). Here the Mayor and Mayoress of Dudley, Cllr Norman Preedy and his wife, meet the Dudley Wood May Queen in May 1960. This was one of his first jobs after being made mayor. Note the open verandas have now been glazed.

ACKNOWLEDGEMENTS

Once again I have to thank all the people of Netherton, and those with an interest in Netherton, who have helped me to compile this book. Many of the people who helped me with the first book have done so again for this second volume. I am therefore seriously at risk of leaving someone out! So, with apologies to anyone who is missing, I wish to thank the following:

Terry Alliband, Janet Armstrong, Jean Bennett, Frederick Bradley, John Brookes, Brian Burchell, Malcolm Cartwright, Owen Chilton, Ann Clark, Lindsey Cooper, Megan Crofts, Roger Crombleholme, Rosalind Cutler, Laura Davies, John Dew, Philip Edwards, Wesley Garratt, Meg and Rob Grainger, Christine Hancox, Wayne Hobbis, Sheila Hodgetts, Keith Hodgkins, Allan Hodier, Joan and Ivan Homer, Pat Hughes, Steve and Jacky Jinks, Jim and Sheila Johnson, Gail Kent, Roy Lea, Erena Little, Sylvia Lucas, Keiron McMahon, John Mason, Sheila and John Mellor, Roger Mills, Jim Morrison, Ron Moss, May Oliver, Brian and Hazel Owen, Frances Palmer, Brian Payton, Jack Phipps, Alan Pritchard, Jane Reade, Tom and Della Roberts, Ken Rock, Lesley Rowlands and staff at Park Nursery, Bob Skan, Alan Smith, Barbara Smith, Geoff and Olive Smith, Janet Stockton, Margaret and Bernard Sylvester, Mrs Taylor, Richard Taylor, Julie Tonkin, Jane Trigg, Dot Tromans, David Willetts, Richard, Jean and Vivian Wakeman, Clarice Walters, Carole Welding, Joan White, Joan Wilcox, David Wilson, Mike Woodall, and the folks at the Bumble Hole Conservation Centre (Sue, Cynthia and Brian), the Editor of the *Express & Star* and the staff at Dudley Archives & Local History Centre.

Special mention must be made of Betty Doo and Joe Guest who had contributed so much to the first volume and who died before I was able go back to them and discuss the content of this volume. They were both very knowledgeable about Netherton and had devoted their lives to Netherton causes.

Once again I must thank Movie Magic for photographic assistance, and Terri Baker Mills for maintaining my 'work–life balance'.

With the opening of the branch library and a clinic, Dudley Wood has expanded to include the post-war development of the Saltwells Estate. Here we see the Sunday School anniversary parade from St John's Church, Dudley Wood, leaving Saltwells Road and entering Bush Road in 1964, led by the Revd Ron Crisp. *(Owen Chilton)*

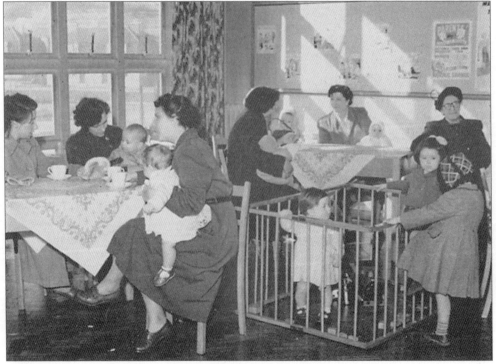

Dudley Wood Clinic opened in the mid-1950s, but has closed and has now been demolished. *(NW)*